CW01239712

Learning from Silence

Also by Pico Iyer

The Half Known Life
A Beginner's Guide to Japan
This Could Be Home
Autumn Light
The Art of Stillness
The Man Within My Head
The Open Road
Sun After Dark
Abandon
Imagining Canada
The Global Soul
Tropical Classical
Cuba and the Night
Falling Off the Map
The Lady and the Monk
Video Night in Kathmandu

Learning from Silence
Lessons from More Than 100 Retreats

Pico Iyer

Cornerstone Press

CORNERSTONE PRESS

UK | USA | Canada | Ireland | Australia
India | New Zealand | South Africa

Cornerstone Press is part of the Penguin Random House group of companies
whose addresses can be found at global.penguinrandomhouse.com

Penguin Random House UK,
One Embassy Gardens, 8 Viaduct Gardens, London SW11 7BW

penguin.co.uk
global.penguinrandomhouse.com

Penguin
Random House
UK

First published in the US as *Aflame* by Riverhead Books,
an imprint of Penguin Random House LLC, 2025
First published in the UK by Cornerstone Press 2025
001

Copyright © Pico Iyer, 2025

The moral right of the author has been asserted

Penguin Random House values and supports copyright. Copyright fuels
creativity, encourages diverse voices, promotes freedom of expression and supports a
vibrant culture. Thank you for purchasing an authorised edition of this book and for
respecting intellectual property laws by not reproducing, scanning or distributing any
part of it by any means without permission. You are supporting authors and enabling
Penguin Random House to continue to publish books for everyone. No part of this book
may be used or reproduced in any manner for the purpose of training artificial
intelligence technologies or systems. In accordance with Article 4(3) of the DSM
Directive 2019/790, Penguin Random House expressly reserves this work
from the text and data mining exception.

Book design by Amanda Dewey

Printed and bound in Great Britain by Clays Ltd, Elcograf S.p.A.

The authorised representative in the EEA is Penguin Random House Ireland,
Morrison Chambers, 32 Nassau Street, Dublin D02 YH68

A CIP catalogue record for this book is available from the British Library

ISBN: 978–1–529–94411–2

Penguin Random House is committed to a sustainable future
for our business, our readers and our planet. This book is made
from Forest Stewardship Council® certified paper.

MIX
Paper | Supporting
responsible forestry
FSC® C018179

*For the monks and nuns, in every tradition,
who have sustained so many of us,
visibly and invisibly, through so many lifetimes—
with thanks and deepest admiration.*

To die—without the Dying

And live—without the Life

This is the hardest Miracle

Propounded to Belief.

—Emily Dickinson

CONTENTS

I
Into the Silence 1

II
Into the World 33

III
Into the Heart 69

IV
Into the Boiler Room 121

V
Into the Mystery 167

Acknowledgments 219

Learning from Silence

Into the Silence

1.

Two men in white robes stand at the end of the road, high above the empty highway. "That fire last October," says one, young and slim, his eyes burning under his shaven head, "it came within three miles of us. At one point our road got blocked and there was no way out. It was radiant."

His older monastic brother says nothing.

"For three days and nights," Cyprian goes on, "the sky was black. Like sooty fog all the time. I went down to the last bench and the whole ocean was bloodred. Plumes of smoke were rising from the hills; I heard trees exploding. It was incandescent."

I don't know what to say. Fire has already left its mark on me.

"You pay for your blessings," I venture at last.

"We do," says the other, burly, with gentle eyes. "A lot of people don't understand that. They see only the beauty."

The beauty, of course, is hard to miss. In the distance, headlands that stretch toward the cities to the south, surf scribbling white around their edges. To our right, a wide expanse of ocean with not a thing to interrupt the blue. A deep valley to our left, and dry golden hills from which mountain lions sometimes emerge, or their prey. Nine hundred acres of live oak, madrona, redwood and desert yucca, a quarter of a mile above the sea.

"I wonder if beauty always has to carry a trace of mortality," I try, and my two friends are wise enough not to say a word, looking out over the charred hills to the promise all around.

IN MY SMALL SUNWASHED ROOM, ten minutes later, I can't imagine death. The sun pinpricks the water through the long windows behind the desk; in my compact walled garden, a rabbit's ears twitch pink, almost transparent. A single white chair sits in front of a low wooden fence, and then there's nothing but brush all the way to the sea.

I set down my carry-on and walk to the desk. For what feels like hours, I can't stop writing, though I had nothing to communicate when I drove up. I stand at last, to see four long pages covered with my scrawl. A bell is tolling behind me, suggesting that barely twenty minutes have passed.

. . .

"You sound like you're in love."

"Exalted, at the very least."

Steve looks at me shrewdly, after I've come down from the mountain; he's known me long enough to be wary of my enthusiasms.

"A love like that can't last. You know that."

"I do. But it can leave you a different person, not always for the worse." He looks away; my friend grew up under the iron hand of priests. He knows that even the loftiest ideas—even the most beautiful spaces—are in the hands of fallible humans.

"What's so special about this place?"

"The fact there's no need of texts or theories. Of anything, really. It's just silence and emptiness and light. No screens at all."

"No screens," he says, registering that I mean something more than television sets. When Steve joined a seminary, his consciousness came so unhinged that he was found walking in his sleep, night after night, and had to be sent home.

"You're not getting religious?"

I look at him. "If you're freed of all distinctions, there's no need of words like 'God.'"

In truth, I'm as surprised as my friend is. Twelve years of enforced chapel at school, every morning and every evening, have left me with an aversion to all crosses and hymnals. In any case, I've never wanted to be part of any group of believers. The globe is too wide, too various, to assume one knows it all.

So why am I exultant to find myself in the silence of this Catholic monastery? Maybe because there's no "I" to get in the way of the exultancy. Only the brightness of the blue above and below. That red-tailed hawk circling, the bees busy in the lavender. It's as if a lens cap has come off and once the self is gone, the world can come flooding in, in all its wild immediacy.

"THE SILENCE OF THIS PLACE is as real and solid as sound. More real, in fact." The words in front of me feel as close as if I've written them. Alone in a shack near the South Pole for five months, the author stepped into a sense of communion with everything around him. Everywhere he looked was a vastness that made his plans and achievements seem very small indeed.

Admiral Byrd was receiving messages by radio from his friend President Roosevelt as he sat in the polar cold and dark; he was the only person ever to have been feted with three ticker-tape parades through New York City. But in his little cell he came to see that success might be another word for peace and peace, at heart, for freedom from ceaseless striving. Though close at times to death, he "felt more *alive*," he confesses, in his solitude, "than at any other time in my life."

His friends in seclusion were moon haloes, the "bright pebbles" of stars, "ice crystals falling against the face of the sun." His greatest enemy, he came to see, was a "discordant mind." He watched a brilliant aurora, he paged through a tale of monastic romance, he sat for long hours in enveloping silence and began to appreciate what T. S. Eliot would call the "life we have lost in living." No human, he saw, "can hope to be completely free who lives within reach of familiar habits and urgencies."

IT WAS VISITING MY PARENTS' friend Kilian, earlier in the week, close to home, that brought the admiral back to me; I'd glimpsed the copy of Byrd's memoir *Alone* beside his chair. For a quarter of a century, none of us has ever seen Kil ruffled or without his air of quiet self-possession; usually his small figure is to be found seated at a terminal, chuckling over fractals. Brown corduroy jacket, gold-rim specs, shock of frizzy brown hair.

I don't think I'll ever meet a brighter soul; he mastered both physics and philosophy at Harvard. But when I moved to Boston, he volunteered to drive with me all the way across the country so he could show me round his old hometown. The one time we stopped, for eight hours in a motel, I awoke at first light to find him at the check-in desk, scribbling across a postcard of bright-eyed raccoons to send back to his two young daughters.

Now, as I look in on him, Gregorian chants fill the space. He's long been drawn toward the wisdoms associated with Asia, but cancer, it seems, has moved him to turn to solace closer to home.

What words can be of any use? I recall my friend has always delighted in Kafka's nutty riddles.

"I just found this unexpected passage," I say, pulling out the worn notebook I carry in my pocket. "'You do not need to leave your room. Remain sitting at your table and listen. Do not even listen, simply wait, be quiet, still and solitary. The world will freely offer itself to you to be unmasked; it has no choice. It will roll in ecstasy at your feet.'"

Kil smiles; sitting still is his only option now.

"I should let you rest," I say, trying not to think that forty-nine years are far too few. "But I'll see you two weeks from now. With the latest news from Europe."

Kil struggles to his feet. Movement is so difficult these days. He shuffles over to hold me, and I realize we have never touched before. I feel his bones through his shirt, so fragile I worry they'll crumble in my arms.

"Take care of your mother," he says quietly, as if knowing that two weeks is much too long to hope for.

. . .

IT WAS ANOTHER FRIEND, Dwight, who first sent me toward silence, thirty-three years ago as I write this. He'd seen me sleeping on the floor of someone's house, my home all ash, and he knew I could do better. Three and a half hours up the coast, he said, and I'd have a room to myself. A bed, a wide desk, ocean views. Lunch to collect from a communal kitchen, two hot showers for anyone to enjoy. No obligations and a suggested donation of just thirty dollars a night.

What could I lose? I got into my dusty white Plymouth Horizon, four days after my thirty-fourth birthday, and followed the interstate freeway to a single-lane highway. Very soon there was nothing to my right but golden hills—a scatter of black cows in the meadows—and nothing to my left but the motionless blue plate of the Pacific. A white lighthouse lonely among the rocks.

Then an even narrower path, barely wider than my car, zigzagging up to the top of a ridge. At every switchback, a heart-stopping view of the ocean far below, the receding coastline. In the bookstore, near the end of the road, a young monk, waiting to guide me down to my room in an unprepossessing line of motel-like doors.

"This is Big Sur," he said, pointing to the heater against one wall. "It can get cold."

A single bed on one side, a rocking chair next to the

blond-wood dresser. Through the windows, the ocean a sheet of fire. The sense of homecoming instantaneous.

SMELL OF ANISE as I walk along the silent road in the sharpened light of late afternoon. Sound, now and then, of surf, sidling in and receding among the rocks below. Flowers the color of blueberry ice cream along the way.

Such a simple revolution: Yesterday I thought myself at the center of the world. Now the world seems to sit at the center of me.

THE SIXTY-MILE STRETCH of coastline along Central California has always felt like liberation as I nose around blind turns on Highway 1, a sheer drop beside me falling to the sea. Groves of coastal redwoods that enfold one in a primal darkness; high cliffs that tumble down, when it rains, toward the water; an ocean unmarked by oil rigs or islands or anything at all. "Here was life purged of its ephemeral accretions," wrote Robinson Jeffers, who left Europe and his classical education to build a stony tower above this coast and hymn the Homeric ruggedness for forty-three craggy years. Here was a "shifting of emphasis and significance from man to not-man."

Henry Miller had just finished roaming around Greece,

sensing gods on every hilltop, when he arrived here in the middle of World War II, settling into a small convict's cabin down the road. He had in time to brave a mile-and-a-half climb down from his hilltop perch every time he needed to collect his mail; he had to gather firewood whenever he wanted a cup of coffee. He carried barely ten dollars in his pocket when he washed up on the deserted coastline; there was no telephone, no electricity, no sewage system in the entire area. Three of the years he spent here, wrote an early biographer, were the happiest of his life.

We can "make our own Bibles," he noted as he looked across forty miles of emptiness, "invaded" by stillness. "There being nothing to improve on in the surroundings, the tendency is to set about improving oneself." The casual reader might have thought the good-natured bum known for scrounging a living among the whores and gutters of Paris an unlikely monastic, but as he gazed across the ocean towards Japan and Tibet, the man with a gift for saying yes acknowledged that "it was here at Big Sur that I first learned to say 'Amen.'"

In 1962 he wrote to the Trappist monk Thomas Merton—they shared a publisher—in response to Merton's accounts of the early hermits of Christianity; Merton—whose books were banned on very different grounds—eagerly wrote back, seeing that Miller's *Wisdom of the Heart* was really little different from his *Wisdom of the*

Desert. The two bald men chuckled over their physical resemblance and Miller congratulated the man of God on having the "look of an ex-convict."

Merton embraced Miller in the opposite direction. The man others saw as a boisterous good-for-nothing had a "real basic Christian spirit," the monk wrote, "which I wish a few Christians shared!" Sometimes it sounded as if the man in robes felt he had something to learn from his secular friend's adventures in the streets. "It is the kind of life in many ways that I was always intending to lead," wrote Merton, of his new pal's roustabout existence, "and did lead to some extent."

"What's the name of these people you're staying with?"

My mother has been teaching comparative religion for decades; she's intrigued, as well as a bit unsettled, by her son's latest discovery.

"Camaldolese. They're the most contemplative congregation of Benedictines."

"Are they open to other traditions?" My mother was educated in Catholic schools; she can still feel the rap of nuns' rulers on her knuckles.

"Very. On the first page of the brochure they put in every room they refer to the Rig Veda. They note that the father of monasticism is the Buddha."

My mother registers surprise, but she cannot forget the Jesuits who came to India disguised as Hindu holy men. "They're friendly?"

"Tremendously. They don't ask anything of visitors other than a 'spirit of quiet and recollection.' Most of the people visiting are women. I don't think many of them are Catholic."

Finally, she gets out her real question. "You're not going to get converted?"

"No fear of that," I say, and she smiles back, knowing her only child well enough to see that he's far too prone to run in the opposite direction.

IN THE DARK—stars whitewashing the heavens above—I step out of my cell and walk up a little rise twenty seconds away, beside the bookstore. I pull open the heavy wooden door. Inside, there's little light save for a single candle in a bowl in one side chapel, another flickering in a thin blue glass on the far side. I sit in the silence of the bare, uncluttered space, everything stilled.

When I emerge, the road looks milky in the moonlight. The globe feels rounded as I've never seen it elsewhere. Stars stream down as if shaken from a tumbler. Somewhere, a dog is barking. Taillights disappear around the turns twelve miles to the south.

Strange, how rich it feels to be cleansed of all chatter. That argument I was conducting with myself on the drive up, that deadline next week, the worries about my sweetheart in Japan: gone, all gone. It's not a feeling but a knowing; in the emptiness I can be filled by everything around me.

I OPEN THE BOOK I've just picked up in the communal kitchen. "One hears, one does not seek. One accepts, one does not ask who gives. Like lightning a thought flares up, with necessity, without hesitation regarding its form. I never had a choice."

I like the fact that those lines were written by the nineteenth-century philosopher who proclaimed the death of God.

2.

THE SILENCE OF A MONASTERY is not like that of a deep forest or mountaintop; it's active and thrumming, almost palpable. And part of its beauty—what deepens and extends it—is that it belongs to all of us. Every now and then I hear a car door slam, or movement in the communal kitchen, and I'm reminded, thrillingly, that this place isn't outside the world, but hidden at its very heart.

In the solitude of my cell, I often feel closer to the people I care for than when they're in the same room, reminded in the sharpest way of why I love them; in silence, all the unmet strangers across the property come to feel like friends, joined at the root. When we pass one another on the road, we say very little, but it's all we don't say that we share.

COMING OUT ONE AFTERNOON into the singing stillness, I pass a woman, tall and blond, looking like she might be from the twenty-fifth-floor office in Midtown where my bosses await my essays. She smiles. "You're Pico?"

"I am."

"I'm Paula. I wrote you a letter last year to see if you could come speak to my class."

She's a novelist, I gather—complete with agent, good New York publisher, grant from the National Endowment for the Arts—and she teaches down the road, two hours to the south. She fled Christianity as a girl, growing up in Lutheran Minnesota, but now—well, now she's been brought back into silence and a sense of warm community.

"Do you write while you're here?" she asks.

"All I seem to do is write! But only for myself. This is the one place in life where I'm happy not to write in any public way."

She smiles in recognition. The point of being here is not to get anything done; only to see what might be worth doing.

THE OTHERS I PASS along the way, or see in the shared kitchen, are not at all the solemn, stiff ones I might have expected. One greets me with a Buddhist bow, another with a Hindu namaste. On the cars outside the retreat-house I read I BRAKE FOR MUSHROOMS, notice a fish that announces, DARWIN. We're not joined by any doctrine, I realize, or mortal being or holy book; only by a silence that speaks for some universal intimation.

"What do you think of this?" an older man asks as we pass one another near a bench.

"Nothing," I say, and he looks puzzled until he sees what I'm about.

"That's the liberation, don't you find?" I go on. "There's nothing to think about other than oak tree and ocean. Nothing to smudge the wonder of . . ." and then I say no more.

We look out together at the tremble of light across the water.

"Do you go to the services while you're there?" asks my Hindu nun friend back at home; she ended up in her convent while looking for the largest empty parking lot in which to protest the Vietnam War.

"I go to the chapel when no one's there." The beauty of the space is that there's almost nothing there as well. Six small windows on either side of the cream-colored walls, their panes painted yellow so light floods gold under the low roof. A large, high-ceilinged, dark rotunda with nothing but a single tiny cross suspended from a majestic skylight, through whose cone-shaped octagonal panels the sun streams down in shafts. Underneath that, a bare concrete block and nothing else.

The strongest image in the simple, intimate space is an Orthodox painting of Virgin and Child, set against a golden background. At the entrance, a picture of three angels gathered around a table at which the last setting awaits a fourth.

None of the heavy wooden furnishings, the icons and gold and fussiness of the churches I grew up among; the Japanese man who designed this chapel knew that little was needed but light.

I DO GO TO A SERVICE ONCE, at Vigils, propelled by a sense of gratitude and duty. Out into the foggy morning—no sun above the ridge yet—and joining a handful of others on the three long blond-wood benches gathered behind eleven chairs in a straight row on either side.

I watch the men in white robes file in from their enclosure, each bowing in turn to the cross hanging in midair, then taking his seat on one of the chairs lined up in front of us.

As soon as the psalms begin, I hear of the "ungodly" and the "filthy," of "licking the dust" and "hating those who hate thee." A metaphor for the struggle within, I know, and the singing is celestial, but soon I'm registering which robes look dirty, which ones clean. I'm counting the hairs in an elderly monk's ears. I'm back on the outside of everything, observer in the worst possible sense.

The instant the fifteen minutes are over, I walk swiftly to the heavy door and out to the large hexagonal window that greets all who step out of the church, its heavy wooden shutters pulled back. Blue above, blue below. A barely paved road bumping down towards the wide expanse of ocean. Rough, red earth and squirrels scurrying across the path. This, I think, is the real scripture, inscribed in all that moves.

As THE DAYS MOUNT in silence, I'm quickly freed of most of my preconceptions. A monk, I see, is not someone who wishes to live peacefully and alone; in truth, he exists in a communal web of obligations as unyielding as in any workplace, and continuing till his final breath.

He's unlikely to want to proselytize; those with their eyes closed in prayer seldom have designs on others.

And contemplation, I come to see, does not in any case mean closing your eyes so much as opening them, to the glory of everything around you. Coming to your senses, by getting out of your head.

On my first drive up to the Hermitage, all I saw was the large cross on the highway, the name of St. Romuald on my door, the crucifix above my bed; as soon as I stepped into silence, all I registered was ocean and sunlight and gold.

Learning from Silence

. . .

"Welcome!" cries the prior, Robert, brown hair neat above his horn-rim glasses, as he passes the bench on which I'm sitting. He waves a friendly hand in my direction and I sense a good-natured, down-to-earth professor whose destiny is to tend to fifteen or so boys, many of whom are older than he is. My cell is a reflection of his spirit, I think: no frills or pretensions, but it has what one needs and nothing more.

Father Robert had been an Episcopalian, studying at Pomona College near Los Angeles, when he saw a picture of the newly opened Hermitage in *Time* magazine. He'd come up here at Easter, in the middle of his last semester, knowing he would stay for life. His adviser, worried, drove all the way up the coast, six hours each way, to try to summon him back, if only in order to take his final exams. In time they reached a compromise: Robert would sit those exams, but from within the enclosure. Now he offers teachings on subjects such as the focus of his thesis, the scientist-priest Teilhard, who knew that humanity is "matter at its most incendiary stage."

Robert's brothers, I gather, are natural successors to the homesteaders and adventurers who were the first to try to make a life here after the unconscionable eradication of Esselen and Salinan Indians. The one who bakes the fruitcake is a professional psychologist who receives calls from the Pentagon to lead suicide prevention workshops and deal with sexual harassment issues; the one I see cleaning the chapel is a scholar, born in Hollywood, whose life was blown open when his mother gave him a copy of *Autobiography of a Yogi*. One has just come from serving the poor amidst the struggles of Central America; another knows how to rig up a pipe platform on a bulldozer in order that electrical wires can be fixed.

No trace of self-righteousness or otherworldliness. "If you think those guys are evil," I hear a monk in the bookstore say as a visitor scans the many works on Buddhism, "we're probably not for you." Even a community of contemplatives needs an infirmarian, a treasurer and a cellarer (to do the shopping).

When the wandering charismatic Romuald founded the congregation, in 1012—it's the oldest continuous one in the Western church—he did not lay down tracts; he simply set up houses of all kinds—solitary, open to guests, mixing men and women—so that everyone had a space in which to find the light within. And when Father Robert arrived here, in the Hermitage's first year, one postulant was sleeping in a barn, and everyone was tending to cows and goats. What would become the chapel was then a garage, and "the proposed rooms for Rev. Father," he wrote, "were lately occupied by brother hog."

3.

As the bells ring for vigils, I awaken to fog. Not a single light visible in the gray. I open my door to head out, in search of company as much as food. Within seconds, I'm slipping on the uneven slope, struggling to stay upright. My flashlight barely penetrates the mist, my shoes are soaked. I slip again and stagger back through the puddles, home.

For hour after long hour, I'm stuck. I can't go out, I can't be still. The heater gasps and groans against the storm; I look out the misted window and see nothing.

Nowhere to hide and nowhere to run. No yesterday or tomorrow. Just a pounding on the roof that refuses to give out.

. . .

I'M ANIMAL AGAIN in the dark. Frogs are burping outside my window; the stuttering heater sounds like heavy rain. Day turns to night, and I see no stars. I search for the comfort of my reflection in the window.

ARE YOU HAPPY to be alone now, some demon might be whispering. Is this your notion of paradise? "Let no one hope to find in contemplation an escape from conflict, from anguish, or from doubt," wrote Merton. The cell is a desert without guarantees.

WHEN I AWAKEN NEXT MORNING, the light is streaming into my little room. The sky so blue, I can't recall the terror of last night.

IMPOSSIBLE, I think, to imagine being healthy when you're sick. Not feasible, when sleeping, to know what it is to be awake.

THE SUDDEN DOWNPOUR is a blessing, but none of us knows when flames will next flare over the ridge. Fire is the true Superior in many a monastery; I think of Merton, walking for hours through the darkened corridors of his monastic home, with flashlight and key, to ensure no embers threaten the aging wooden building in which he and his brothers live. It's hot in the midsummer dark, especially in the furnace room; he looks in on the fuse box, never guessing that his own death will come, fifteen years on, through the kind of fire known as electrocution.

"Sooner or later the world must burn, and all things in it," he knows. Yet he also knows that the monk's first duty is to keep the fires within alight. "If you so wish," observes one of the Desert Fathers whose sayings Merton collects, "you can become aflame."

I SIT IN MY CELL and watch the shadows lengthen across the wall. The sun is sending fireflies scattering across the sea. In my life below, I'm so determined to make the most of every moment; here, simply watching a box of light above the bed, I'm ready at last to let every moment make the most of me.

The world isn't erased here; only returned to its proper proportions. It's not a matter of finding or acquiring anything, only of letting everything extraneous fall away. There's no such thing as dead time when everything is alive with possibility.

4.

SOPHIA DOESN'T LOOK LIKE MUCH. It's one of the two fading trailers set apart from the unprepossessing row of nine connected rooms where most retreatants stay; visitors are allowed to take possession of it not for a week, as with the smaller rooms, but for a month. Logos, the prize trailer on the property, sits below the retreat-house, close to the cliff's edge, ready for takeoff, so it seems, into the wide blue space below and above; Sophia is tucked into a hillside, not far from chapel and bookstore, reached by a steep, barely paved slope and a worn path through the grass.

Inside is a kitchen and bathroom complete with shower; outside, a creaking terrace, overseeing nothing but brush and ocean. Thanks to the quirky logic of monasticism, I can stay in this self-sufficient space for twenty-five dollars a night, where for the far more basic rooms above, I'm invited to offer thirty.

The pipes in the bathroom look ready to give out; a sign, as in all the guests' rooms, reminds us that the plumbing is so ancient here that we have to be economical even with toilet paper. The mops and umbrella in the closet might have been left by an eccentric bachelor uncle who's never had much time for the niceties of a settled life.

Yet it's pure liberation to sit within Wisdom for three weeks. I stash two broken suitcases in the closet, filled with books and the least presentable clothes I own. I make my bed with the sheets and blankets set out for me, unpack the little bottles of shampoo I've smuggled in from some faraway Marriott. Tea bags, too, and chocolate-chip cookies to complement the yogurts and fruit and salad left out in the retreatants' kitchen up the road.

On the desk is a folder welcoming me to the place and a little laminated card on which Romuald's Brief Rule is written out in calligraphy. "Sit in your cell as in paradise. Put the whole world behind you and forget it." If your mind wanders, don't fret. Simply "empty yourself out and sit waiting."

On a table some kind stranger has left me a basket filled with tubs of jam and sachets of cocoa powder; a sprig of holly pokes out from a bottle of balsamic vinegar.

With nothing to distract me, the intimacy overwhelms: the flowered napkin on the kitchen counter is a touch on the arm; the presence—the scent—of whoever was here this morning envelops me in the shower.

. . .

ON THE WALL, there's a small map, and a reminder of where to go when an alarm sounds for fire. No idle threat in a remote settlement with only a narrow, precarious road connecting it to the highway far below. The first monks had been here less than a year when the most important building on the property burned to the ground; seven years ago, another fire again forced a sudden evacuation, with none of the monks knowing if they'd have a home to go back to.

FOR THE MOMENT, though, it feels like the safest place on earth. Nothing stirs, most of all in my overactive mind. I watch a plump yellow moon rise above the hills. Venus pierces me from the indigo sky. I pull out a postcard and write to a long-forgotten friend.

Such moments come every day, I know. But usually I'm stuck in traffic when they arise, or standing in a long line at the airport. On hold for hours with AT&T. It's never possibility that's not present; only me.

"ISN'T IT SELFISH," I remember my old friend Kristin asking, "to leave your loved ones behind to go and sit still?"

"Not if sitting still is the only way you can learn to be a little less selfish."

Learning from Silence

. . .

AS THE MONKS go about their ordered lives, I start to set up my own private rites. I take off my watch as soon as I arrive. I arrange books on my shelves so I can let impulse choose which one to read. I wipe myself clean of any sense of obligation, as I seldom do even on holiday. In a place of absolute trust, I even trust myself.

One morning I pick up the book I'd promised Andrew I'd write on; moments later, I fling it into my suitcase so I'll never open it again. The world can survive without my dead words on a dead text. I think of that friend I've been arguing with in my head and see only the aging parents he's trying with all his heart to support. I sit down to write a lecture and then hurry out to greet the call of sunrise.

BACK IN TOWN I look at the lecture I'd finally dashed off, in response to an unwanted assignment. It reads like love song and hymn all in one.

"IT MUST BE so great to be away from the phone and the TV," my friend Mark says when I try to explain to him the sense of emancipation and delight.

"It's not just that. It's something positive, invigorating." You don't fall in love because of an aversion.

"You're probably glad to be away from other people."

"No; I'm really glad there are others there with whom to share the silence." I pause. "It's more, I suppose, that I'm glad to be away from the self I am when other people are around."

AS I HEAD OUT AGAIN, into the sun, I pass Paula once more and we fall into conversation: so much in common in our professional lives, but all we wish to talk about is something more essential.

"I heard about your fire," she says. "It must have been terrible."

"It was a shock." I can still feel myself inside that oven, my mother's cat panting and struggling to breathe in my lap. One minute we had been sitting in our family home, the next we were surrounded by walls of flame five stories high.

"I seem to remember you were caught inside of it?"

"For three hours. I was lucky to survive. The only thing that saved me was a Good Samaritan." I see the shirtless figure on our empty mountain road, poking a hose from the water truck he'd driven up, to try to be of help, towards every new approach of flames. I feel myself wheezing, as when an attack of asthma convulses me, not even thinking that a car might be the least safe hiding place of all.

"I'm sorry," she says.

"Thank you." I look out at the mist moving swiftly up the slope, now revealing the blue-green waters below, now concealing, as if playing games with a diaphanous scarf.

"Was it losing everything that brought you here?"

"I don't think so. But"—I look out again—"it did clear the way for many things."

EVERY DAY IN SILENCE is an incarnation and sometimes I feel I'm walking through an allegory as I step out of Wisdom and head in the direction of the Nacimiento Road, or the Road of Birth. Everyone stands for anyone. That woman seated on the grass beside a bench, the pages of her diary flapping over. That other, in deep converse with a monk, as they disappear around the far turn. The man walking away from me in golden light as if clothed in flame.

I, too, no doubt, anonymous to everyone I pass—a happy liberation for someone who's so often wanted to be different and original. When I scribble lines here, I'm fairly sure they're the same lines that almost everyone around me is writing.

ONE AFTERNOON EVERY WEEK, I drive down to the unsheltered pay phone in the parking lot of the motel at the bottom of the hill: I can't neglect my responsibilities in the world altogether.

At my feet, a turquoise cove, white frothing against some rocks. All around, sharp blue sky, a flood of golden poppies on the slope. I call a friend in the Hollywood Hills, to send her greetings on her birthday, and her husband answers, buried in a script he's writing for *Star Trek*.

"Why are you calling?" he asks at last, unable to ignore the shine in my voice. "Just to gloat?"

How to put words to it? As easy to catch sunlight inside a jar.

I REMEMBER, after my last stay, taking a card I'd written in the silence to the post office. Rereading what I'd written before putting it into the slot, I'd been surprised to encounter "faxes on my desk." Only two days later did I recall: I'd been writing of "foxes on my deck."

MY LAST MORNING IN SOPHIA, I speed around the room, gathering all the trash to take up to the two big cans by the side of the retreat-house. I rinse and rub my plates till they shine, wipe down every square inch of desk and chair and toilet. I make a pile of the novels I've read, to give to the monks; the books on spirit I'll donate to the communal kitchen.

Learning from Silence

. . .

ALL CHORES COMPLETE, I sit out in the bright sunlight before lunch and the long drive home. I remember—jogged, perhaps, by my talk with Paula—accelerating down the road under our burning home after those hours in the midst of flames, houses smoking on every side, the shattered hulks of cars littering the way. I'd had to call my mother, away in Florida, visiting her nephew, to tell her that all her fifty-nine years of photos, of keepsakes, all her jewels and lecture notes were gone.

"There must be something."

"No," I say, "it's gone, all gone. Everything we owned is ash."

Then I'd driven to a friend's house to sleep on the floor. Before I did, I asked if I could use a computer; my job at the time involved writing back-page essays for *Time* magazine, and I'd just had a front-seat view on the worst fire in California history.

My small piece ended with a poem I'd picked up in Japan; intuition seemed already to be reminding me that no event is simply good or bad.

My house burned down
I can now see better
The rising moon.

Into the World

1.

In love it often feels as if we're glimpsing the hidden architecture of the world: no convergence is coincidence and every moment seems to observe a hidden logic. Everything makes sense and life becomes a shining web of correspondences.

But how long does such a vision ever last, and what can we do when it subsides? Fire illuminates a life quite brilliantly, but in that very blaze it threatens to bring down everything in its path.

I'm thrilled, in the wide-awake silence, to sense that all the scattered filaments inside of me come together in a singing whole. I'm reminded that the best in us lies deeper than our words. Yet two or three days after I'm back in my daily life, second thoughts begin to nag at me like summer flies. I'm not a monk, and never will be, so what exactly am I playing at in my borrowed cell? My longtime girlfriend is awaiting me in Japan; she and her two small children count on me for emotional as well as financial support. My poor mother has been brought back to ground zero after the wildfire; she needs me nearby more than ever.

These days of sunlight can only be a means to gather a candle to carry back into the unlit corners of my, or any, life.

PAULA, whom I met along the road, works hard to sustain what she's found in the Hermitage down in the tumult. She sets out a place in her garden where she can sit quietly every day; she tends to olives, to chickens and bees, points out to children and students the whirring of bluebirds. In her free time she drives up to help the monks with building projects and odd jobs.

The first time she came up here, she tells me, she'd just lost her father. She stepped into the chapel and saw Father Robert washing the feet of his brothers. A longing she hadn't known she had was answered.

FOR MY PART, my job calls on me now to cover the Summer Olympics in Barcelona. I'm responsible for writing on all twenty-six sports on offer. But—prompted in some fashion by my days in silence—I head away from the cacophony of the International Broadcast Centre and start to follow the Bhutanese team around what looks to them like another planet. The four teenage archers have never seen a high-rise before. A subway station becomes a thing of wonder. The harbor itself, to visitors from a landlocked kingdom, a miracle.

There's something unfallen even in the midst of a global spectacle, I'm reminded, surrounded by flashbulbs and TV crews broadcasting the action to 169 nations. When I come back from the round-the-clock festival, I find a desk piled high with credit card bills, glossy magazines, petitions. In their midst, barely visible, the four-page newsletter that arrives every season from the Hermitage.

In one corner, the brothers have made a list of what they need most right now.

POTS AND PANS

EUCHARISTIC VESTMENTS

INSULATION FOR REFECTORY/DINING ROOM

SUPPORT FOR EDUCATION OF MONKS

The simple, shadowless request rings through me like a bell.

Learning from Silence

. . .

THE NEXT TIME I'm sitting in silence, I drive down in the bright afternoon to the pay phone along the highway to check in with my sweetheart, Hiroko, in Kyoto.

"Where are you now?"

"The Hermitage."

"I think so. Your voice so different."

"You can hear it?"

"All light."

Then, so faint I can barely hear her over the crackle, "If you meet another woman, no problem! I can be more, more excellent. But how can I compete against a temple?"

FIVE WEEKS LATER, I surprise us both by flying across the Pacific, to start a new life with her and her son and daughter in the tiny apartment she's rented in an anonymous suburb. There's so little space in the two small rooms that I have to sleep on a couch next to the TV; the only place to work is the desk that Sachi vacates when she goes to elementary school every morning. To my friends—to me, two years ago—this might look like a prison; now I can see how luxury is defined by all you don't need to long for.

"Anyone can sit in a Zendo," a monk down the road has written. "The trick is to sit in the world."

2.

"WE ALL WANT TO DISSOLVE," the old Zen monk in red bobble cap and thin glasses tells me, with a wry chuckle, as he greets me in the chill mountains behind Los Angeles, three hundred miles south of Big Sur, where I've come at the end of December. "We all need the experience of forgetting who we are. I think that's what love is: forgetting who you are."

He flashes a crooked grin. "Forgetting who you are is such a delicious experience. And so frightening."

Bells toll through the dark, and I hear the sound of clappers. The stooped figure leads me up an unlit path between the trees to the meditation hall. The smell of incense everywhere, as thirty students dressed in black take their seats in rows on either side of a central altar. Not a cough or tremor.

When they break, they hasten out into the night and

walk in single file between tall pines on the icy ground. Upon their return, to the sound of a pounding drum, they recite the Heart Sutra, at lightning speed, its syllables, in Japanese, a mere fusillade of sounds.

For seven days and seven nights, they'll mostly be sitting in this hall, stepping out occasionally for visits to an outhouse and meals taken swiftly and in silence, mopping the leftovers with tea.

In his small cabin—ALL FRIENDS ARE WELCOME, says the mat outside—my gracious host, twice the age of most of his comrades, assures me that there's nothing special about this training; this cluster of cabins in the high dark mountains behind L.A. used to be a Boy Scout camp (though now, in his mordant telling, it's a penal colony). Every word and action in the emptiness decisive as a slash of calligraphy across blank pages.

TOWARDS THE END of the next day, my guide to Zen practice leads me up again through great shafts of light between the conifers. The air vibrates with the intensity of silence. We step into the room where the head of the community, a tiny eighty-eight-year-old Japanese man in heavy, layered robes, is sipping something strong.

"I came to America to die," the abbot announces. "I arrived when I was young: fifty-five. I was fit as a jumping shrimp." He's never bothered to learn much English;

words are needless scratches on the clarity of what lies beyond.

I look at the monk who's brought me here. I think of myself, at seventeen, in the little hotel in Bombay, listening over and over to his songs about Marianne and Suzanne, the one who told you when he came he was a stranger.

Always in command, on point; and now, on this dark mountain, he carries himself like an anonymous grunt, scrubbing floors, cooking for the abbot, driving the old man to the doctor.

He has no interest in holy men or golden sentences, he says; he knows how to play that game a little himself. This is simply the most helpful—the most imaginative—response to the predicament of life that he has found.

"Here you find answers," I suggest to Leonard Cohen shortly before I leave.

"Here you find freedom from answers," he replies, in the grave and gravelly baritone beloved by many. "Freedom from questions. A landscape without doubt."

THE SONGS, I realize as I drive down from his mountain, are often about suffering—panic and jealousy and pain. He never pretends he isn't defeated, by love and himself and all the ways in which he isn't what he hopes to be. But they're never simply sad. They speak for a struggle in which words like "happiness" and "sadness" are beside the point; the only thing you can believe in, he keeps telling us, is a reality you can't comprehend.

IN MY TRAILER AGAIN, above the ocean, I feel a storm approaching. The wind is shaking the roof of the bathroom, the trees are shivering outside. I look out my window and see the exodus begin: the line of departing cars might be exiles hurrying to the train station as the troops approach.

What to do? Join the other vehicles on the road, and abandon the one shelter I've found, my best preparation for life? Stay, and run the risk of being stranded here for days? Paul's Slide a thousand feet away will soon begin slipping into the sea. Boulders the size of church bells will cut off the road to north and south. Trees may fall across the highway.

I have that article to transmit, that lecture to give. My mother, alone in the large house she's rebuilt halfway up the mountains. The world to which I owe obligations.

Thinking about tomorrow will only take me out of paradise. I sit where I am and face a truth that can't be outrun.

ALL NIGHT, THE RAIN. The wind howling in an extravagance of pain. Branches banging against the roof. A ceaseless drumming on the tiles; drip-drip-drip from every eave. A sigh and a cry as the windows shake and the bones of the old structure ache and groan.

Near where I shiver, the heater stutters. The rain subsides and the silence is absolute.

Then the downpour resumes and the heater sputters once more against the chill.

WHEN I EMERGE, hours later, it's to find the sky rinsed clean. Panels of turquoise, aquamarine, azure down below. "We are never tired," Emerson reminds me, "so long as we can see far enough."

I'M SINGING TO MYSELF when I walk out again, towards the farthest bench. Repeating, under my breath, the one phrase that keeps coming to me here: "Thank you, thank you, thank you." I used to think that the act of prayer was about saying, "Please."

By the time I head back down into the world, three hours later, I feel immune to everything. I'm taking the curves fast and, without thinking, singing along with the only music I can listen to when driving out of silence, Van Morrison. "Be thou my vision, oh Lord of my heart . . ."

As I arrive on the highway, I have to turn off and stop,

to record a thought. Again. Then again. I might be a sunlit river overflowing its banks.

Back home, I pull open the curtains and set up a folding table next to my window so the light floods through me. I roar through two weeks of emails, barely stopping to catch a breath. My poor friends at the other end must be perplexed, but maybe they'll be grateful to meet someone they never see otherwise.

Invoices, confessions, invitations: a torrent of beseechings and commitments. That series of blogs you promised to provide, someone writes. "Oh, that's just some crazy idea young Stephen dreamed up to make us seem up-to-date," I reply. In my haste I somehow copy poor Stephen on the message.

Two days later, the realization: what does it mean to sit in silence if it leaves me, at least for my first few hours back, less attentive, less thoughtful—more cruel—than I'd ever hope to be?

"I don't understand it," says Kristin. "You've always sounded so happy with your life in the world."

"I was. I am. That's why I couldn't remember what I was missing."

She looks at me sharply. "I guess it's a relief from all the travel. To be in one place."

"The travel is interesting. It keeps me in touch with the lives of others. The relief comes in getting to be one self."

Or no self at all, I want to say. Then I catch the look on her face and decide to talk about the Lakers game last night.

EVERY MORNING IN MY SECRET LIFE, over toast and tea, I reach, by instinct, for a book. Marcus Aurelius, the Roman emperor counseling himself on the battlefield, reminds me that the world is our stepmother: not really where we came from, but the force with which we have to make a future. Pascal, the man who created a kind of calculator and proved that vacuums exist in the world, tells me, "I never thought a sense of peace and the passion of fire could reside in the heart at the same time."

At college, introduced to Henry Thoreau, I'd been shaken by his call to solitude: here was a man with the courage to step aside a little from regular society and live at an angle to the norm. The rare soul ready to shape his days in accordance with an inner account-book and not the external spreadsheet that convention tends to encourage.

What I was too young to see then was that being alone was never an end in itself; it was the means to becoming a more useful member of society. "I have no private good," the seeming hermit wrote, "unless it be my particular attempt to serve the public." He was known around town as the guy who fixed people's ovens, painted their houses, advised them on their beans; when Emerson took off on lecture tours, it was Thoreau who looked after his friend's wife and kids for as long as ten months at a stretch, amusing them all with jigs. He took pains to build his cabin in the woods within sight of his neighbors, right next to the railway tracks that would in time send twenty trains a day roaring past. The title of his first talk at the Concord Lyceum was not "Solitude" but "Society."

Some people say that Thoreau was a hypocrite to return to his mother's house every Sunday for dinner, to entertain visitors to his cabin on Saturdays; I see it, more and more, as the whole point of his experiment. "I think that I love society as much as most" is one of the central lines in *Walden*; "I am naturally no hermit." The book he wrote during his two years, two months and two days in the cabin was at heart a love letter to the older brother who'd just died in his arms; at its center is a twenty-three-page ode to friendship so soaring one might never wish to be alone again.

PUTTING HIS BOOK DOWN, I slide back the screen door and step into the dusk. The best time to take a walk not only because of the flaring, munificent light of the magic hour—

every bush burning as colors seep across the sky—because it can feel as if the whole world is slowing down as it prepares for rest.

The grace of this place is that it makes me see everything as I might a loved one when asleep. At peace in that rare space where, as Meister Eckhart has it, "one has not been wounded."

A doe steps out of the monastic enclosure and starts to graze on the grass below the chapel; I leave her to herself while I walk along the road, rabbits scuttling through the undergrowth as quail scurry towards their resting place.

When I return, two other deer have joined her, stepping out of shyness to nibble in the gathering dark.

"Do you believe in God?" a friend abruptly asks, after I'm back in the world.

"It hardly matters."

"It does to the people who open their doors to you."

"It does to them. But for me it's like asking if I believe in this room, or in you."

A pause.

"If you come upon something that feels real—this moment—belief doesn't really come into it."

"Hunh," she says, having pegged me already as slippery.

Learning from Silence

. . .

SOMETIMES IT'S ALMOST UNSETTLING, how completely the memories overwhelm me in the silent room. At home, they emerge in fragments, stabbing moments on the freeway or as I'm hurrying from one appointment to the next; here I'm possessed by them, in every pore, suddenly walking up a steep street in the city named for peace, watching the bowler-hatted women make their way to the plaza outside the cathedral, goods on their backs in rainbow-colored bags. Wandering along the carless Malecón in Havana, hearing the boys shout as they splash among the rocks under the seawall.

Seeing two forms rise and fall, shadows, on the wall of a hut; my hand on your mouth, the collapse of your long, soft hair.

"SENSUOUS": I've heard that the word, more alive here than anywhere I've been, was coined by sightless Milton.

ONE DAY IN LOS ANGELES I meet a woman with the bright, open face of an angel. She's full of facts, laughing, but I sense in her a sweetness so absolute that she's set up barbed wire on every side to protect herself. She chatters away in giddy flights, and I can't help but feel that she's trying to hide something tender and more real.

"I wonder if you'd be interested in this place where I go, up north?" I have no wish to inflict my choice on her; nobody can share a love, and in any case we all prefer to come to epiphanies on our own. "But if you're free sometime," I say, "you might want to try it."

She does have time and she asks if she can come up on some occasion when I'm there, to show her round; a monastery sounds forbidding, an all-male territory of people living by very different rules.

"Of course," I say. Months later, I prepare myself for her arrival.

On the day in question, there's no sign of her car, making its way around the turns on the road snaking up. Nothing in the parking lot. I go out to the bookstore when it closes, and find a map left out for her by the monk on duty, his handwritten "Welcome!" fluttering from the door like a butterfly.

Later, under starlight, I look out. Nothing. I barely sleep all night. When I go out again before dawn, there's no sign of her slow and overcrowded SUV.

At last, close to twenty-four hours late, I see the dust-begrimed white car laboring around the turns, and come to a loud halt in the bookstore parking lot.

"You risked it!" I say, sensing that the delay arose from some sudden apprehension. "Why don't you settle in and then I can show you around?"

An hour or so later, a soft knock upon my door.

We walk up the short slope and across the parking lot, now bare, and I pull open the heavy wooden door to the chapel. Reflexively, we part and make our separate ways across the gold-lit space.

I see her sit down on a pew, look around. I retreat into my favorite side chapel to give her time alone. At moments I catch her reflection along the rotunda wall.

When we emerge, her face looks flooded. We walk towards the closest bench, and she clutches at her heart.

"Are you okay?"

"Sorry. It's just—I mean, I'm moved."

We sit on the bench, let the silence gather. Just here is where the ocean below pools around rocks and turns, as nowhere else, a milky green.

"Were you surprised?"

"Completely." She shakes her long fair hair, as if shivering. "Moved. So happy I can't speak." For a few moments, no words at all. "So affected," she goes on. "Deeply affected."

Then I hear a harder edge. "But I could never be alone here. Where you'd be in your element." She lets the words settle. "Where you find your truest self, you're happy. I envy that."

By the time I turn to her, her eyes are thick with tears.

3.

My mother doesn't say a word as we drive away from the pretty red-roofed, white facility, St. Francis; when we saw the line on the screen above my father's bed flatten out, she signed the papers without a word and thanked the men in black who came to take the body away. In her gold silk sari, she looks as serene and elegant as ever.

The minute we get back to the new house on the mountain, however, she strides into her bedroom and tears off all her bangles. She flings the gold across the room. Whom to be beautiful for now? The only man she'll ever love—since the age of seventeen—is gone.

I look in on her and she waves me furiously away. I'm the one, I realize, who'll have to organize the memorial service, notify friends and family. Pen the obituary, receive with a smile the flowers that appear at the front door.

Early one morning, when I know a friend will be keeping my mother company, I go out into the predawn dark and get into my car. I drive up into the mountains and cut across the pass, towards the even narrower highway that leads to the path that snakes up the hill.

I get out at the top, back in the Hermitage, and the silence enfolds me. I sit on a bench and look out over the ocean. Behind the wash of traffic, the steady sigh and recession of the sea. From down the road, a bell tolls for Eucharist.

I stay there for two hours, doing nothing. Then I drive three and a half hours back along tight switchbacks, ready to face the world.

AS SUMMER ENDS—Fire Season's meant to be over—the plumbing for the entire community gives out. Lightning scratches through the skies. Just after Lauds, plumes of smoke shoot up, seven miles to the south. Weeks later, I learn that nine fires were set off by the electrical thunderstorm; six are contained. For a long while, every corner of the area is dense with smoke. The sun burns orange in the black sky. Helicopters, many of them military, start drawing water from the lake above the enclosure and dropping it at two-minute intervals. Ash falls like snow.

Within an hour, nineteen monks are told to evacuate; seven remain, along with a friend and two workers, to try to protect their home. The others are driven to an inn in Carmel, ninety minutes away, where a friend of the community puts them up. They observe Vigils and Vespers, the Eucharist in the motel's public areas; they marvel at a dishwasher. As a report in the Hermitage newsletter will have it, "We all thought it would be a great idea to have one of these at the Hermitage."

For many long days they stay there, cooking and cleaning, observing all their usual Offices. For seven weeks the fire keeps blazing, a threat to no structure in the twelve-hundred-square-mile expanse except the monastery. The damage across the region comes to eighty-eight million dollars.

When the convoy of five cars pulls out, taking the monks to safety, the tough-seeming guys on the bulldozer crew shed tears, I hear, and not only because they've grown so fond of "Mom's Coffee Cake," baked by Brother Bede.

I RECEIVE REGULAR UPDATES on this from a lay monk across the country who's following the drama closely from his own retreat-house. He'd written a letter to me, years before, after reading about a book of mine with "monk" in the title. Then, three thousand miles from his home and fifty-five hundred miles from my apartment in Japan, we'd walked into one another along the monastery road in Big Sur and he'd come down to my trailer to chat.

Aelred is a sturdy soul, bursting with energy and delight. He's set up his own one-person hermitage, complete with Japanese dry-sand garden, on nineteen acres in the hills of northwestern Connecticut. He writes hymns—by the dozen—sometimes drawing from the Vedas. In his letters, as in his presence, he all but overwhelms me with his enthusiasm.

Now, in an exquisite card graced with a Chinese painting of a lotus, he tells me that he heard a few monks stayed behind in Big Sur to protect their home as the flames drew closer. His own place is safe, he writes, but he's down to 117 pounds, and there's no cure for the AIDS that some of his Christian colleagues are saying is a form of divine retribution. He's living with his mother now, unable to care for the space that has for so long been his central love. "Friends look after the grounds," he assures me, "and we maintain our monthly zazen sittings. Nonetheless, it's disorienting to be away from my life's work."

More than a hundred of his poems are about to be published—"my labor of twenty-five years. So I have this to look forward to. I hope you are enjoying the persimmons and the Nara autumn."

A FEW WEEKS LATER, another card from the address I've come to know so well, though this one arrives without elaborate calligraphy. It's from Aelred's mother, reporting that her beloved son passed away peacefully only two weeks after he'd written to me. The fires had still been raging then, but he'd received the book I'd sent him, on the subject of hope.

4.

A MONK IS AT HEART the ultimate man of the world. That's where his sense of kindness and self-sacrifice is most needed, and it's to those in trouble that he must attend. He may deepen his commitment in private, but it's on the streets that he has to reap the blessings of his practice.

One brilliant October afternoon, in the foothills of the Himalayas, I step out of my little room and walk away from the three-story, whitewashed Tibetan building where I'm staying. I cross a barely paved path crowded with vendors and beggars. Men call out offers, their brothers extend hands. In the large leafy courtyard within the central temple, young monks in red robes are seated on the ground while colleagues come at them with slashing challenges: "If the self does not exist, who is it who's asking this?" "If what you see is just a mirror, what lies behind the mirror?"

Then through a security building and into an antechamber and I enter the bright, thangka-filled room where

I've been visiting the Dalai Lama for more than twenty years. The dominant colors are red and gold. The large picture windows look out upon the deep Kangra Valley, ridged snowcaps in the distance.

The man who bustles into the room has been a monk since the age of four. But in uncommonly specific and urgent ways, his destiny is in the emergency room. Yes, he tells me, perhaps—*perhaps* (he stresses again with a scholar's caution and precision)—some in his tradition have had the chance to practice meditation to quite a high degree; but when it comes to caring for those in need, the poor and suffering, they need to learn from their Christian brothers.

Buddhists, I think, are experts when it comes to defusing the suffering in the mind; the Christians I know are often deeply attentive to the suffering in the world. Neither, however, can pretend that pain can ever be entirely healed.

His answer to my every question is arrow-straight. When I ask him about his achievements, he remembers not the Nobel Prize, nor any great global honor, but just one dispossessed soul he met in Soweto, the township in Johannesburg. Growing up under apartheid, the man had confessed to his Tibetan visitor that he had no hope, no belief he could do anything. He couldn't vote, he couldn't get a job; he couldn't even aspire to freedom. They spoke for about an hour, the Dalai Lama tells me, and at the end he really felt he'd imparted to his new friend a little confidence. "Today," he'd thought, "I made some small contribution."

"What is the saddest thing that's happened to you?" I ask, and, instantly, he's looking out the window, completely lost to me. He's at the border with Tibet, thirty-seven years before, bidding farewell to the horsemen who have accompanied him on his fourteen-day flight to freedom as they turn around, to go back to their homeland and, almost certainly, their death.

Fifty years meditating on the cure for suffering, but no physician can afford to misplace his heart.

RETREAT, I'm coming to find, is not so much about escape as redirection and recollection. You learn to love the world only by looking at it closely, in the round. I'm too inclined, I sometimes think, to accentuate the positive, so as I come out from the Hermitage, I try more and more to take myself off to the wounded or desperate parts of the globe. It pains him, I hear the Dalai Lama say, to see an animal killed on TV. But it's going to get killed anyway, and maybe by watching he can learn something.

In Port-au-Prince, women are relieving themselves along the main road, near a shack on which is written, "Centre de Formation Intellectuelle." I pass a clinic, and am greeted by a sign, in two languages: "Arms Prohibited Inside."

Before I even leave the airport terminal, blood is streaming from my hand, in the rush to retrieve bags from the shuddering carousel. My bag in any case hasn't arrived, so I'm advised to return the following day to see if it's come in on the next two-hour flight. Heading back to the airport twenty hours later, the car that's taking me gets violently rear-ended.

The average person here, a doctor tells me, is dead by the age of forty-four; one child in ten never makes it out of the ward. Three hours' drive from the Hermitage, excited software engineers are talking about living till one hundred and fifty and remaking the world by doing no evil; in Haiti, as I jounce along its own Highway 1, all I can see along the wide, unpaved expanse is a row of tombstones.

On Sunday, when I step into the church at the broken heart of the city, it's to meet an explosion of bright colors. High-spirited greetings, smiles and unembarrassed waves. Music blasting as freely as in the streets. On the first day of January, the drummers and singers who give concerts in my hotel, as revelers wave their guns about, invite me to come with them to the beach so we can greet the promise of a new year.

IN THE ABSENCE OF MATERIAL comfort, of course people turn to faith, a friend who knows Haiti well explains. But the celebrants I see in the church there, like the people I watch filling the pews of Addis Ababa on Christmas Day, the nuns gathered around the ruins at Angkor, are not responding only to need; they haven't forgotten that something exists beyond the grasp of our ideas.

I'm lucky indeed to have the time and money to go on retreat, I know, a luxury that most might envy. But riches are not so simply defined. Traditionally, the historian R. H. Tawney reminds me, humans were spiritual beings who, for prudence's sake, took care of their material needs; nowadays more and more of us are material beings who, for the sake of prudence, attend to our spiritual needs.

5.

WHEN NEXT I SETTLE into the blue-and-gold silence above the sea, it's to hear a bulldozer protesting as it goes back and forth along the slope down the road. The beep of its heading in reverse, the shouts of men anxiously directing it.

Inwardly, I curse. Do the monks really need to make this place more crowded? Might it not imperil the silence that is the Hermitage's greatest gift? Many of us would happily contribute to their coffers if that might save them from having to build more trailers.

TWO DAYS LATER, I can't remember quibbling like a spoiled child. The bulldozer, the shouts, that cabin coming up down the dirt road from where I sit: they're all as much a part of the silence as the birdsong.

Learning from Silence

. . .

"When one keeps quiet, the situation becomes clear." The celebrated existentialist sounds almost like a Taoist as I pick up Camus's essays in the uncluttered stillness. "Everything is simple. It's men who complicate things."

Through the mist, I hear the sea far below. Stars blurring high above. Down on the highway, a string of red lights edges towards the nearest turn; then a string of white, as the long line of cars is turned around at a roadblock and forced to go back the way it came.

A dim beam halfway up the hill, now visible, now not, following the curves of the monastery road: a monk, I'm guessing, back from the week's shopping two hours to the north.

In celebrating the beauty of what's around us, Camus writes, each of us "surrenders to his god the small change of his personality." Our real fortune lies in what belongs to everyone. Yes, he assures me, "there is a higher happiness, where happiness seems trivial."

Camus's wisdom arose from never forgetting the power of sunlight. He grew up in poverty, he often writes, in the industrial coastal town of Oran, in Algeria, but in another sense he was always rich; he and everyone around him had light and water and sunshine at their doorsteps. He was born with blessings that his friends in the gray classrooms of the Sorbonne envied. "Even my revolts," he confesses, recalling his boyhood, "were brilliant with sunshine."

His upbringing likewise instructed him in honoring the invisible. "I lived on almost nothing," he writes at one point, "but also in a kind of rapture." He clings "like a miser to the freedom that disappears as soon as there is an excess of things." I look around me—the wonky room, the squeaky terrace, the wide blue grandeur in the distance—and think: No house to maintain, no phones to answer. No noise to block out, no traffic to navigate. I can bring every part of myself to every moment. "I wanted to change lives, yes," Camus wrote when young, "but not the world, which I worshipped as divine."

His deepest gift, always, had to do with finding the confidence to affirm: "The great courage is still to gaze as squarely at the light as at death." His enduring lesson was that the difficulty—the irrationality—of life need not rob us of our joy. That Sisyphus's efforts will always be fruitless need not mean that his life is wasted. A plague can awaken heroism and compassion precisely because we're no longer sleepwalking through life. Camus was killed in a car crash, at forty-six, only fifteen months after being awarded the Nobel Prize. Yet it's hard to think of his life in terms of anything but lucidity and light.

BACK IN THE SILENCE above the sea, I walk across to the retreat-house and notice that the slopes leading down to the farthest cabin have been entirely cleared of brush, thanks in part to the bulldozers, to make way for two new structures and to keep all flames at bay. For the first time ever, the hill is a flood of unembarrassed gold.

TWO DAYS LATER—again—the rain. The Old Testament as close to me now as the New; the law of love cannot efface the law of judgment.

When the downpour subsides, I pick up the worn book inside my desk and, almost at random, read, "Look, the winter is past. The rains are over and gone. Blossoms appear through all the land."

APART FROM THEIR RETREAT MINISTRY, I've learned, the monks support themselves through their celebrated (brandy-soaked) fruitcake and bookshop. Beyond that, they rely on donations. One man bestows on them his very old Ferrari, and assures them that they can get sixty thousand dollars for it. Others volunteer time working at the store, and the man with the gaudy pink hotel down the road offers help in resurfacing the road free of charge. A brother of one of the monks makes a six-figure contribution every year to help keep the place afloat.

Then, however, he dies, and the money is gone. A friend of the Hermitage promises a graphic accelerator so the monks can continue their studies of German and Hebrew online. Two years later, it has yet to show up.

EVERY TIME I make the steep drive up the hill, I'm bringing fresh perplexities. Our daughter, Sachi, has been diagnosed with cancer and is spending an entire year in the hospital; my mother, on this side of the Pacific, has told friends that she wishes she could have thrown herself on the equivalent of her husband's funeral pyre. How can I begin to tend to both, and be in two places at the same time?

I watch the other retreatants walk slowly along the road in the last flare of light, faces for a moment golden, and wonder what questions they have brought to sit with in the silence.

The friend who introduced me to the place had learned about it from a colleague. The colleague had been through a devastating divorce and didn't know what to do. Finally, on instinct, he decided to come and spend a year in the company of the monks, helping them with chores around the property.

Near the end of his year, he received a letter from his ex-wife. She was about to receive her degree. Would he like to come down and celebrate her graduation?

He did so, and when she saw him, she saw again the man she'd fallen in love with. All the stress in him, the bitterness, was gone. She invited him home and they picked up their lives together as before.

IT DOESN'T ALWAYS HAPPEN like that, I know; it can't. But there are so many ways of finding release from the prison of the self. Every time Sachi stirs in the night, Hiroko is up in an instant, and by her side.

IN THE STURDY new fortress my mother has rebuilt in the hills, the reverse 911 calls keep coming, season after season, telling us we have to evacuate right now. Too often, as soon as the sun begins to decline, the winds pick up till they're roaring around us at up to ninety miles an hour. The doors of the new house rattle, the beams creak; it seems unlikely we'll see another morning.

I head on one such evening into our library. I sit at the desktop that Kilian so kindly set up for us before his early death. I place the huge stack of handwritten notes I've scribbled during my days in silence beside me, and start to type them in to our computer, while the windows shake and the lights in the room flicker, threatening to give out.

I hear the slow crash of ocean against rocks as I transcribe my notes and then the wash of withdrawal. I see stars emerge from behind clouds in silence, pinpricks as from a sewing machine in the heavens. I watch a hooded figure running through the dark.

Days later, as I walk through the knife-sharp light of late afternoon, back among the monks, I might be passing through an illuminated landscape. I'm stepping between raised letters and what could be illustrations, of robed figures against an indigo sky, in front of a forest called Los Padres. The Fathers. At the old oak near the picnic bench—perfect spot for a party of one—I see the whole valley open up beside me, so that now there are high mountains on one side, and still the ocean on the other.

A car rattles past towards the turn, and then stops. I see a gaggle of rough figures inside: new workers, I assume, I have yet to meet.

"I don't mean to scare you," says one, poking his head out the window. "But I think I saw something walking behind you."

"Very close?"

"Not so far."

"What do you think it was?"

"It could be nothing," he says. "But there have been sightings around the property."

I recall the little notice pinned up in the communal kitchen: if you see a mountain lion, try to make yourself as large and loud as possible.

A curious injunction for those of us who have come here to become as small and invisible as possible.

Darkness falls fast as I hurry back to my cell and, as never before, bolt the door behind me.

Into the Heart

1.

"Here's the one who's always alone!" exclaims the woman helping herself to quiche and salad in the communal kitchen as I walk in; she's red-cheeked and glowing with life. "I've seen you along the road." She's in her fifties, I'm guessing, a decade older than I am, and has the welcoming air of a full-throated nun who just happens to be dressed in civvies. "Why don't you come down to my place? We can have lunch together."

I'm tempted to scurry back to my immaculate silence, but it's hard to resist such infectious warmth. She comes here every Easter, my new friend explains, as I dole out soup from a huge tureen. To catch her breath a little. Her job across the country involves teaching emotionally disturbed boys. "We used to have only murderers," she goes on with a smile. "But now it's any boys who've committed a violent crime. The murderers were easier."

Ree, as she introduces herself, leads me down the slope to the faraway trailer named for the Word. It looks like a weekend cottage in Tuscany. A hammock swings between the trees; there's a picnic table on the sunlit lawn and honeysuckle climbing the wooden pillars around us on the deck. She bustles off to fetch pretty place mats for the table and we take our seats with the ocean beyond.

"So how did you first come here?" she asks.

I tell her about the schoolteacher friend who assured me that even fidgety teenage boys calmed down after two days in silence, as if they'd found their truest home.

"I was working for the Lake Placid Olympics," she tells me in return, "back in 1980. As marketing director. And I was talking to this guy I was having a brief fling with. An FBI officer." She lets out a guffaw at the absurdity of it. "We'd just made love on top of a mountain and he said, 'Where are you going to go when this is all over?'"

"And I said, 'Big Sur.' Without thinking. It just came out of me. So we traveled across country, to Carmel, and my last day here, I thought I'd better go down to Big Sur to see why I'd come. So I drove south."

Her telling is exquisitely paced; she knows just how to hold a room of restless teenagers. "And most of the people in the hills then were growing marijuana. So they'd look at you like, 'Don't come here!' And I saw this big cross by the side of the road and I thought, 'Whoever's here isn't going to be growing marijuana.'

"In those days, no one knew about the place. There wasn't a single guest staying. And the food, you can't believe how lousy it was! I asked the monk on duty, 'Do you have to be religious to stay here?' 'No,' he said. 'You just have to like beauty and silence and solitude.' I thought, 'Beauty I can handle. Silence and solitude? I'm not so sure.'

"Now I've been coming back for eighteen years."

"You're Catholic?"

"I wasn't then. Now"—Ree pauses—"now, I'm a Roman Catholic Buddhist. But I'm beginning to think that's not broad enough."

MY CHEERFUL LUNCH in the sun brings me out of my cell: I so cherish the rare sense of joy and peace I find when alone here—I'm so wary of complicating the spell—that I'm more of a recluse, the monks tease me, than any of them might be. But our chat has affected me in a deeper way, as an alarm clock might. Often, Ree tells me, she goes to the bookstore to talk to the monk on duty. Not because she's feeling lonely or restless, but because she worries that he might be.

I smile at my double standards: if ever I come across a piece of wisdom from some exotic or faraway tradition—Sufism, say, or Buddhism—I eagerly transcribe it. As soon as the same words come to me from the culture I think I know well, I turn away, imprisoning myself within my prejudices.

I think of my father, so bright-eyed and alert the last time I saw him, a tower of books by his chair, as ever, waiting to be devoured. One month later, he was gone. My mother, taking a well-earned week away, only to hear the phone ringing and be told that she'd lost everything she'd accumulated over almost sixty years in a wildfire. Silence speaks to me as no scripture ever could; it brooks no argument. But to learn a little about companionship, compassion—about living with impermanence, and even dying—perhaps it's to the men within the enclosure that I should turn.

NEXT MORNING, as I go up to the kitchen to fetch some fresh milk, I walk into a throng of monks crowding the parking lot that's usually deserted. All of them are wearing body-length scarves—in two cases crimson—and they're gathering around a small tree. They're passing out olive branches to the guests who trickle in around them, and to the workers from the cloister who amble up; two brothers, in hooded white gowns, sport reflecting shades against the strong midday sun.

Then every last soul is handed a candle, the candles are lit and the entire group proceeds around the property singing hosannas, as a German shepherd bounds out of the enclosure and starts sniffing at monastic ankles. I follow the others into the chapel, as if by instinct, and before I know it, I'm caught there, watching the gentle, gracious Guestmaster play Pontius Pilate as the Passion of Jesus is reenacted.

At the moment of the crucifixion, all the monks fall to the floor, heads down.

One of the older brothers, a former prior with the snow-white beard and withdrawn air of a mystic, steps up to the lectern and begins to speak, about the mystery of the week, the procession into the heart. The progress, day by day, deeper into the midst of what we cannot fathom. The voice of this sometime chemist, after fifty years in this place, is so soft I have to lean in to catch the clenched poetry of his aria.

When he concludes, the monks proceed into the rotunda, the rest of us following. As shafts of light flood down, they offer, to the tune of a single strummed guitar, a sweet conjoined hymn of praise.

At the end, each one embraces his neighbor and says, "Peace be with you." The smell of incense from a swinging censer sanctifies everything. Glints of silver dapple the wall from the strong spring light outside. As the others head into the refectory in the enclosure for a hearty communal Palm Sunday feast, I hurry back to my trailer to meet the auspicious occasion alone.

Learning from Silence

. . .

HOURS LATER, walking along the empty monastery road, I round a turn to see a young-looking monk with a trim blond beard and an open face: the one, I realize, whose paintings fill the bookstore. They're portraits of the world that moonlight as prayers: A sun showering gold across the ocean. Stars above pines in a silent night. Slopes rich with violet and orange running down to deep blue waters.

"You know"—I stop him as he nods—"your art is now the gift I share with friends across the world."

My hope is that he'll stop and chat, and so he does, pointing towards a nearby bench, where he sits down to disclose a little of his story: a happy boyhood in San Francisco, followed by long years of investigating Buddhism. At one point, his questions took him to Assisi and there he felt so pierced by light that he was moved to take on Franciscan robes.

For some time he worked with emotionally troubled kids in Chicago. But then his solemn mission retreat brought him here, and he realized that painting itself might be a kind of service; perhaps he could reap the fruits of contemplation in art while sharing in the "witness of community"?

"Most of us came here in our forties," he says, and he doesn't need to explain more; they'd worked through various options in the world, as well as their illusions and boyhood romances. They knew what they were getting into, and what they were giving up.

That didn't mean that they could leave the world behind.

"We bring it with us," he says, speaking of stress, of acceleration and dividedness. "And sometimes it can be more intense here because it's more internal."

He hears what I'm not saying, too. "There are lots of people doing this same work out in the world. Hermits, recluses, hermitesses. Doing it while they're in business, raising families. There can't be a therapist in California who hasn't been here!"

"Journalists, too," I say. The place was just on the front page of *The Wall Street Journal*. NBC called up last week. I might have questions about the punky kid strutting around in the black "Hidden Rage" T-shirt—he's here for *Travel Holiday* magazine—except that I'm no different.

"Still," he says, as we get up to go our separate ways, "our prayer rhythm calls us back to what's important."

MAYBE—I'm back in my room now—one kind of asceticism comes in the letting go of certainties, and of any notion that you know more than life does. And one form of sacrifice involves listening to the tradition you thought you knew inside out.

Learning from Silence

. . .

AFTER DARK I HEAD into the chapel—I count on its being empty at night—only to find a hooded figure, all in white, alone on a barely visible bench at the back of the rotunda.

Then I discern another figure, behind the cross, in the darkened space. I walk to the side chapel, where I kneel before a candle, saying thanks.

As I continue around the space, following its walls, I catch glimpses of the hooded figures, motionless in the candlelight.

When I step out again, a cat rubs itself against my legs. A light rain begins to fall.

AS HOLY WEEK UNFOLDS, I'm drawn into the ascending rhythm of the hours. I step into the chapel once more, next night, and see, as before, outlined figures, unmoving but on alert. One, now, is in a different position against the wall, as if he's shifted from four o'clock to five on his silent passage around the Stations of the Cross.

He burns the air with all he's keeping in.

NEXT MORNING, clouds hurry up the slopes, ghosts rushing along a nave. I make out a woman, through the gathering fog, kneeling on the tarmac as she walks along the monastery road past the chapel. One evening later, Father Robert is washing the feet of his brothers, a reminder that he's as much their servant as they are his.

NO BELLS ON GOOD FRIDAY: just a steady dripping in my sink. Every crucifix draped in white. Candles snuffed. A large wooden cross at the heart of the rotunda, on the floor. I look in, after Vespers, and see a lone monk seated beside the fallen crucifix as if beside his brother's body.

NEXT DAY, in the unbroken silence, the chapel is a song of flowers. A single candle shines inside a cement-block cross.

FINALLY, looking past my petty preferences, I join the monks for lunch on Easter Sunday, right after Eucharist, shamelessly skipping the service and walking around to the refectory just as a couple dozen bodies emerge from the chapel and walk over to the small entrance hall to stand in a line and pile plates high with rice and vegetables.

In one corner of the room of six-seat blond-wood tables, cakes and more cakes; Easter eggs. In another, cans and bottles of every kind of nonalcoholic drink.

Next to me is Father Joseph, the first Chinese brother in the 980 years of the Camaldolese congregation; he was a Salesian in Italy, wrote a thesis on a German theologian, is off soon to lecture at the University of Beijing while completing a book on Taoist-Christian mysticism. The number of languages he speaks exceeds the number of bodies at the table.

A monk from South Africa comes over and joins us. "There's a writer from my country," he says, "beautiful, who says of the African veld, 'There's so much silence, you can hear the stars move.' That's how I feel here; last night, I heard the stars move."

Father Robert—I see him always as a teacher, passing on what he's learned from the mystics with an uncle's fondness—explains how it's permitted to transfer from a less contemplative order to a more contemplative one, but not the other way round.

"Does that mean contemplation is closer to heaven?"

Before he can answer, a younger monk comes by, arm in arm with a smiling young woman. "Father, we have an announcement."

"Oh, no!" cries the good-natured prior, beaming. "We've had too many announcements!" He turns to the woman helping herself to corn beside him. "You have two children, isn't that right? Well, I have twenty or so."

AFTERWARDS, joining the monks to wash dishes—already they're moving briskly towards their next task of the day—I hear the one who's always looked a little gruff singing as he douses the plates in boiling water. I'm carried to another world.

Another monk, relatively new to the community, confides, "You have to learn how to enjoy leisure. To do nothing and be peaceful. Because leisure is where things happen to you.

"But you can't be leisurely for just half an hour. It's only in the sixth half-hour that things start developing inside you—and then you have to know you have another three hours to go."

"It sounds like writing," I begin, and then stop: nobody's life depends on what I do.

BACK IN MY TRAILER, I feel uncharacteristically choked up. How many more weeks will I get to spend in this place so joyous and so calm at once? How many more times will I see these sweet-tempered souls, many of them already gray-haired and a little stooped?

2.

Nothing ahead and nothing behind, the sea erased in the heavy fog. I've bumped along the dirt road that runs between the private trailers, down to the cliffs, and then up again, to the highest of the new cabins, the one named Hesychia, or Inner Peace. My little Toyota bounces around potholes, wheels spinning in the dirt; I almost smash my head against its low roof.

The rain is so heavy I have to tuck my shoulder bag under my thick green sweater as I clamber up the wooden steps. Whoever has been here before me has left a piece of paper propped up against the window, reminding me that I am myself the secret chamber that I seek. Quite perfectly, the last line has been blotted out—the rain, I assume—so the author is Anonymous.

. . .

ON THE COUNTER, a ring of lipstick faintly kisses the rim of my mug; as so often, I feel closer to whoever was here this morning than to myself.

INTIMACY, I think, can be such a treacherous thing in the world: whom are you getting close to, and with what intent? Here it's only the opposite—distance—that can feel like profanation.

THREE DAYS WITHOUT a word and then the rain abates and I walk out onto the damp, empty road. I hear a sound behind me and a dusty white Isuzu pickup pulls up; a trim man, compact, in his early sixties, with neatly combed gray hair parted on one side, steps out. John is one of the workers who's been living here for years, helping the monks with duties around the property; though none of these lay residents wear robes, most seem washed clean by the silence they've chosen to live close to. John's words emerge as clear and precise as those of the monks at the bookstore cash register.

"You know," he says, perhaps because he always sees me taking the same walk, "there's a small beach a few miles to the south? After a storm you can find sand dollars there, these great white dollars, with emblems on them. You come upon pieces of driftwood, jade."

"I was just reading, in Thoreau, how a man will go out of his way to pick up a silver dollar on the street. But he'll walk past golden words without a second thought."

John smiles. I say things here I'd never dream of saying in my regular life.

"It's just this big white beach," John continues. "Across from Pacific Valley School, where forty of our children go. It's where they shot some of *From Here to Eternity*."

"Our children," I notice, from a man without kids. His words themselves like sand dollars, gathered along the shores of his quiet home.

John's been to Argentina and Brazil, I recall from an earlier conversation; he once lived in the Virgin Islands. Nowadays, he drives ninety minutes to the north to Trader Joe's to buy Chilean wine for the monks. "They go for that wine," he'd told me. "I know because I do the recycling here."

I say goodbye and walk back to my cabin. Ten minutes later, a shy knock on my outside wall: John, with a bag of candies, and a label from the fifty-five-acre vineyard he once owned, Fair View Farms, two hours to the south.

ON CONE PEAK, in the distance, there's still a layer of thick snow. Sting of cold wind, lights across the hillside.

Bells ring for Vespers, and forty minutes later I follow a trail of elegant new lanterns, worthy of a five-star resort, up the slope to the chapel. A full moon above me in the rain-washed dark.

I make my way to the side chapel and kneel beside the candle. I hear the heavy door open, and soon the whole space fills with the sweetest singing.

The sound of carefree joy: a young woman, I presume, delighting in her freedom.

When I get up to leave, I follow the circular walls around, counterclockwise, and as I make my way, keeping to myself, out towards the front door, I catch sight of the singer: it's the small, grizzled monk of sixty-eight who barely speaks, he's so deep in adoration.

I HEAR IN HIS VOICE the sound of all he's giving up. By choice, of course, and yet obedience can be an unforgiving master.

The real meaning of conversion, I read, is "continuous renewal." A promise that has to be made again and again, and again.

3.

IN THE QUIET OF MY CELL, I never tire of the outstretched hours. Days without plan are days without fret; I feel as if I'm doing nothing here, but when I go over to pick fresh tea bags out from my suitcase, I notice that its upper compartment is bulging with pages blackened with my scribbles, an overfull stomach. I see, in its main section, the books I've finished reading and wonder how I can go through two or three a day when it feels as if I'm doing nothing but taking walks and writing long letters to pass along the peace.

Luxury indeed to follow whim; my conscious mind can argue me out of any belief and into it again. Pure joy to inhabit a world whose dictionary has no place for "worry" or for "strife." I recall the day I flew across the ocean after hearing that my father was in the ICU; as I stepped into the small hospital room, I realized that my bank account, my resume, my business card would none of them be of very much help at all. The only thing that could sustain him—or me—would be whatever I'd gathered in stillness.

When I step into the bookstore, the monk on duty is on fire. His grin so wide, it could light up the entire hillside.

He greets me with delight—we'd met over lunch—and then, as if unable to contain himself, says, "Coming here gave me the courage to die. I went home"—across the world—"and I quite literally died to the life I'd known." For more than twenty years he'd been traveling all over, as a priest, giving six Masses on Sundays, crossing distances of four hundred miles in a day, living, for a decade, in a Zulu village with almost nothing; now that energy is brought to an explosive pitch and he hardly knows what to do with it.

Of course, he says, there's a honeymoon period when you tumble into a love like this. "But I've been here eight months now and still I feel I'm on honeymoon. Every morning I wake up and touch my forehead to the ground. Can this last?"

Can it indeed? The monks are committed to being invisible; a single burning flame in a room of tiny candles can act like a shout in a world of silence.

I'VE MADE IT my practice now, on every retreat, to select a book, almost at random, from the monastery store. In my usual life, I'm hostage to my choices, my professional needs; here I can let something wiser alight upon a book for no reason at all.

Browsing quickly through a few of the titles on display, I come upon one that seems to speak for a very devout faith: hope, its author writes, is not a belief in happy endings, since our imaginations are likely too limited to see what is happy in the end; it's simply a sense that there's an order to things, that they make sense, even if no sense that we can fathom.

I take the book back to my trailer and for two days it becomes my constant companion. It's only when I get to the very end that I receive a sudden shock: the author turns out to be someone very well known to me—our magazine's bureau chief in Beijing, whose reports on the economic reforms of Deng Xiaoping I distilled and rearranged week after week for four long years.

I put the book away, shaking; one secret life opens out upon another.

"I FEEL THE SPRING so powerfully here," I say, when I join the monks for lunch again, and one of them passes me the salad bowl. "Really, as I've never felt it before. Maybe because there's nothing to distract me from the flowers and the birds."

"It's all subjective," says the man with the hood across from me, and I recall that he's just been speaking about abuse, his alcoholic father, the need for closure. "For me, going to Detroit is like that."

He pauses, not wanting to abrade. "It can be hard for us to smell the flowers."

Another monk takes his place beside me at the small blond-wood table. "They say there are several steps to becoming a monk," he tells me, "and it takes ten years to do it fully. Initially there's euphoria; then the plateau, where I am now. Then the dark night of the soul." He pauses to take a bite. "When you enter a world as different as this, you can't help but meet the shadow. Like in *A Passage to India*."

There's silence at the table.

"All this stuff comes up," he goes on, perhaps knowing I'm his only audience. "Issues of sexuality and Eros. In the world, you get inured to it, there are so many images all around."

"I suppose you're alone in the dark with your thoughts here," I say. "And your longings. Every prompting hits you like a gale-force wind."

"Precisely."

A monk comes by with orange juice, another points me towards a cart loaded high with tubs of ice cream. The salad and bowls of pasta brighten the uncluttered room; light streams in from the long, high set of windows open to the garden.

"When I go out into the world," volunteers one of the brothers, "I feel like a sea anemone."

"A CNN enemy?" I say, encircled in my own preoccupations.

He smiles. "A little creature of the sea. You know how sensitive and tender they are. If they trust where they've been placed, they open up. Put them in a harsh environment and they close very quickly."

4.

In the open expanse of a spring afternoon, I walk, as Ree has urged, right into the monks' private enclosure, along the dusty driveway, and past a row of cottages: each one a cell, hidden behind a high wall, with a garden in front, and cinder-block surfaces. Then I head up, past rusted cars and the little huts, the battered silver trailer where the workers live, at the back of the property. Up, past ponderosa pines, for almost an hour, to the body of water that comes to the brothers' rescue whenever flames flare up, and a picnic table where a monk is stretched out, head raised to the sun like a lion on the savanna.

Startled, he smiles a welcome and gets up from his rest. "Let me show you something." He's dressed in shorts, as for the bush, and wields a long stick.

"Watch out!" he cries as we begin to walk. A few feet ahead of us, a small snake. "A baby: they're the dangerous kind. They don't know how to rattle."

"It really must be Eden here," I say; there are serpents everywhere, and much of the brush is poison oak.

Deep within the trees is a platform somebody has constructed with ropes and branches, from which we can look down at the cluster of cells far below. An Indian grinding-stone. On the surface of the lake, mallards and lily pads. Up above, on a lonely ridge, the bungalow belonging to Jack, who tried to get a visa to live for three years in a cave near the Dalai Lama's home in Dharamsala.

As I take my leave of the monk, abashed to have disturbed him in his privacy, and start to head down, past slopes of flowering mustard, another truant hurries past, climbing towards the lake. "This is the way to heaven?" he cries. "There's glory at the top!"

I smile at the extravagant words. All self-consciousness gone in a place where self disappears and consciousness comes to seem as vast, as enveloping, as the ocean all around.

WHERE ARE SUCH PEOPLE in my daily life? I wonder, back in my trailer. Everywhere, comes the answer, but I can't see or stop to hear them. I'm too caught up in my own schedule, my seeming busyness. Like someone who plays the radio all the time and claims never to hear the sea.

. . .

NEXT MORNING, as the fog lifts, I have the sense I often have here, of seeing the world at the moment it comes to life. I recall looking down at the twenty-five pods gathered around the bell tower and the refectory, tiny against the hillside and the huge expanse of sea beyond; they looked so frail I wished to say a prayer for them, as for a newborn in the not always easy world.

So orderly, too, in their hopeful human arrangement. Like the redwoods in the valley beside them: each with roots five feet deep, but intertwined, so the health of one depends on the health of every other.

AS THE YEAR DRAWS towards its end, back in my mother's house while the town around me draws its shutters fast, I call my monk friend from Mount Baldy, Leonard; when we met he'd been living by the monastic name his abbot gave him, suggesting the silence between two thoughts.

"How's your teacher?"

"Radiant. He's fifteen years younger than when you saw him."

Then, since it's a day of worship—sometimes known as celebration—I drive across town and up the thin, quiet road that leads to a Japanese-looking temple commanding a view over the ocean far below, and maintained by American nuns who've joined a Vedanta convent. The silence stands to attention the minute I step out of my car. There's a polished sense of alertness, of something poised and cleansed. Not a mere absence of noise but a living presence, as of glass walls erected by years of prayer and devotion.

I sit on the steps outside the meditation hall, in the clear winter air, and open a biography I've been reading in the trailer named for inner peace. "Once you have been turned round," Ludwig Wittgenstein reminded himself near the end of his life, "you must *stay* turned round." Relapse can be so easy.

"Somehow I always get my car washed when I drive up there," I tell the one friend who's become a fairly regular visitor to the Hermitage. "Which is funny because, as you know, I never usually wash it."

"I do the same," he says, surprised.

"I stop muttering to myself there," he goes on, "because there's no one to listen. I can't get angry." Then he stops. "All these notes you take when you're up there. Are they interior?"

"Yes, but only because I feel it isn't me. Usually, if I write personally, it's about someone called 'Pico Iyer,' of a certain age, with a certain background. There, the personal feels impersonal. The I is part of some larger I. Writing about myself feels like writing about everyone. In fact it's writing about the external world that feels most interior."

"I know what you mean."

He looks out across the crowded restaurant.

"I sing aloud when I'm there," says my friend. "And not only to scare away mountain lions. I become kind of a dork. 'It's two miles down,' this monk was saying as he walked toward the highway. 'And how many miles up?' I said to him.

"I write all these letters, too. And what I say is so open and generous. And when I come down, I'm shining with light."

"Just the words you'd never use in your regular life."

He laughs. "I count the paces to the farthest bench. Eleven hundred and seventy-nine. I hid a little something for you there. Check it out the next time you visit."

THE TWO OF us get together every December because both of us are often on our own then: my old friend has yet to find the right woman and I leave my family in Japan to keep my mother company over the holidays in her lonely house in the hills. Often working for the same New York magazines, he and I find ourselves living on planes and in hotels for weeks on end. My pal flies so much, he once won the ultimate frequent-flier prize: unlimited trips for thirty days across the world on Pan Am. When I visit him in Chicago—an empty apartment thirty-two floors up—the only thing in his refrigerator is undeveloped film.

In the Hermitage, however, he sees that Nowhere is much more interesting than anywhere. He becomes impish and sensual and calm. "I talked my dreams into a recorder, but when I came down, I heard only this strange man muttering.

"And that stranger's who you really are."

IN THE BRIGHTNESS of an April afternoon, I hear a rap on the wall of my trailer; I open the door, and a shining face glows at me in the sunlight. I've come to know the most gregarious of the monks through chats in the bookstore, and I sense an overflow on his part that is crying out for release.

I put the tea bags he's brought into a pot and we talk about the novels we've been reading. About places that we love; he used to travel widely. About the challenges in the life, and all that I can't see in my sunlit silence.

"The Tibetan tradition is strong," my friend begins, "because they have an entire community around them. Supporting their practice." He stops to sip some tea and nibble on a cookie. "The thing with us is that we're swimming against the tide. We can survive only if we go deep within—learn to be instead of just doing."

"That's your particular mandate, isn't it? To deepen community through the fruits of solitude?" The Camaldolese are the rare monks who don't sleep under the same roof. But I've noticed how the chairs in the chapel face one another, as if to remind the men of where their obligations lie.

"I really think you're the true counterculture," I continue. "Living on the edge. Without many resources, alone with doubts and fears. Didn't St. Paul say something like that? 'In hope we are saved, but hope is not hope if its object is seen?'"

The solitary passage through the monastic dark, night after night, sounds merciless. "I was just seeing my spiritual director," my friend explains, "and he told me I had to give up my family. Give up all my ideals! Get rid of my dreams and truly give myself over to the community.

"I was stripped naked! When I came here, I had three pieces of luggage. But after he stopped speaking, I had nothing at all. He took everything away from me."

He stops, as if to collect himself. "Give up my ideals," he goes on. "I think he saw that as something I was holding on to, so I wouldn't give myself entirely to the other monks here. Something I was hanging on to, as a way out."

"It sounds like Merton."

He smiles. "It does indeed. In the Eastern tradition, the abba is a spiritual director, who tends to every monk. But in our tradition, he's more of a manager—a managing director, really. So it's the practice that becomes our spiritual director. But it's difficult to have only the Rule to turn to."

We sip our tea. "I can say all this quite happily to you now," my friend explains. "But when he said it to me, I was in a state of shock. I was ready to drop everything. I'd been told, before I went home, only to see family. Not friends, because they'd expect to see me every time. And any time I want to see an ailing parent, I have to ask permission. Often it's not given."

He shakes his head. "It's a hard discipline. You can't give yourself any leeway at all." Then, above us, the bell begins to ring, and, getting up, he hugs me for goodbye.

THE QUIET OF my cell vibrates with all he's said—all he hasn't said—after he departs. But then I remember another monk, whose conviction seemed as clear as a flashlight on a moonless night.

I'd met him along the monastery road one day, and given voice to what I'd been thinking. "It must be so hard to die to all your hopes. But I suppose that's what your life is about: a preparation for death."

"Yes," he'd said, "we do have to prepare for death. But

I adamantly believe that this isn't first and foremost a training for death. It's a training for life. It's teaching us how to live."

He'd looked away for a moment, and then back at me. "The longing itself," he'd said, "is the ecstasy."

5.

THERE ARE SIX OF US, waiting to get into the little van as it pulls into the parking lot of the mission, off the fifteen hundred mile interstate. The road to the Hermitage has been cut off by winter storms to the north and to the south, but the monks have organized a "shuttle service" to bring friends in once a week, through the back Nacimiento Road, which cuts over the hills and empties out very close to their entrance.

A small, quiet monk in his midsixties is at the wheel, with a pointed gray beard and sharp, piercing eyes. A trim blond woman from the Bay Area settles in next to him and asks, "How long does it take to get there?"

"I don't know," he says, staring ahead of him. "I'm not too good with time or dates."

. . .

As he begins steering us through an outstretched army camp and then along a thin road across a dense valley, shafts of sunshine lighting up the foliage, I recall that this is one of the most fervent of the monks, and therefore one of the most reserved; it's only obligation—obedience— that has brought him out into our midst.

"I remember once," he says, "I was staying in the trees, in a cabin for two weeks. Just before I left, I saw splinters all across the ocean. There wasn't a ripple in the sea, so it must have been whales, a hundred of them or so."

Twenty thousand swim past every spring, I've read; on the beach down the road, dozens of elephant seals are stretched out like tumbled boulders. Whenever torrential rains close off the highway, more and more barriers between natural and human worlds dissolve. Deer are seen walking along Highway 1; I awaken at times to the barking of sea lions. All of us so tiny, we feel part of something huge, and a little bit less mortal.

"How did you end up at the Hermitage?" the woman in the front seat asks our shy driver as he steers.

"I was reading an article in *Time* magazine," he says, blue eyes scanning the road, and his words coming out clear and perfect. "On monasticism in the U.S. A friend suggested I read it. And something happened. I can't say what it was. It was just one picture, of the three they had on the page. Of the Hermitage. I knew."

"The same little article that summoned Father Robert."

"That's right." He stops to concentrate on a passing car. "Suddenly everything that repelled me was all I wanted."

"It's wonderful you can choose your vocation like that."

"I didn't choose. He chose."

A heavy silence falls.

"I've seen boulders as big as cars come down," the monk goes on, perhaps sensing the need to move to safer ground. "Some of the brothers have seen rocks forty feet wide."

"You get snow at times?"

"At times. One time we had snow several feet deep. Two of the brothers built a snowman outside the refectory."

I remember again why every visit feels like a renewal.

"Father Isaiah mentioned that he was driving one night," the monk continues, "and he saw a dark shape running beside the vehicle. Then it just bounded onto a rock and disappeared.

"The next day there was a dead deer by the road."

. . .

As soon as I'm safely in my cell, I'm an impulsive child again, stepping out into the starlit quiet and spinning myself round till I feel dizzy. Nothing feels forbidden here because there's no one I'm supposed to be.

Then I walk up towards the chapel, following the small beam of my flashlight, and shiver as I see a dark figure, approaching from the other side: myself, I realize, reflected in the flashlight's glow.

Inside, the place is shriven, chaste; on the floor, I spot a tiny scrap of paper. I bend down and make out words scribbled in a very small hand: "I wish to know and be kinder."

A NEW PRIOR is now in residence, and Father Robert has returned to the order's urban house in Berkeley to teach, and, perhaps even more, to give his successor room to breathe. Nothing essential ever changes here, but the surfaces, the beams and pipes and gasping vehicles, are always in need of renewal. I recall how Thoreau begins *Walden* with a chapter called "Economy" and it's almost eight times longer than the chapter called "Solitude."

When I step into the chapel now, I walk atop blue skies and flowering trees; there's a new reflecting surface on the floor. A small wood-encased fountain, encircled by lavender and sagebrush, sings in the monastic courtyard. In my cell there's a pane of glass placed above the long desk, so I see red flowers and the sun every time I look down as much as when I look up.

The new boss is blessed with the unlined, smiling face, the thick hair and broad shoulders of an NFL quarterback. He used to work with Cesar Chavez in his marches for social justice. Now, as Washington takes the country to war again, a little sign saying PEACE appears down on the highway, and all-night vigils fill the chapel; the monks take to fasting every Wednesday and donate a tenth of all their earnings to children displaced by the fighting.

One day I look in on a service and hear my fellow retreatants join the monks in calling out prayers for everyone to support. One man is hoping for a good outcome from his parole hearing; another prays that the Church be as tolerant as possible.

HEADING BACK TO MY CABIN—the world a festival of green while water keeps dripping off the roof—I come upon a small shopping bag placed on the hood of my car. Inside, another shopping bag, and inside that, two Typhoo tea bags and a CD of Russian Orthodox music that (an accompanying card explains) "sounds like spirit soaring." Also, some small texts, including the Rule of Benedict, that are handed out to friends of the community.

My monk friend who came to tea, I realize. The card he's left shows Winnie the Pooh walking with Piglet.

"I don't feel very much like Pooh today," says the good-natured bear.

"There, there," answers Piglet. "I'll bring you tea and honey till you do."

I SIT DOWN, and a wasp starts buzzing around me. All day long, worrying and fretting. Next morning, I find it overturned, by the sink, legs wriggling in the last throes of death. I don't know why it moves me so. Has it banged itself in fruitless longing against the screen window all night long? Failed to see the opening I left so it could escape?

For no reason I can muster, I lift it into a tray and take it out into the sun, as if that might help it die in peace.

THAT NIGHT, exultant at the end of mist, I walk out, under a blue-black sky, brandishing the broom I now take with me in case of mountain lion encounters. On the notice in the kitchen about such creatures, one visitor has scribbled, "Sighted, August 22," and another, "Seen near the bench by the trash-cans."

A small elderly monk, sporting a black beret, walks past me on the road, heading up the hill again. Then he stops.

"Excuse me? Have we met?"

"I think we've passed one another on this road, for years."

"Excuse me for asking"—his eyes are bright and merry—"but I was wondering what you were planning to do with that?"

A broom is not often seen in the wilderness.

"I know it looks silly, but I was told once a mountain lion was stalking me on this road."

"Ah," he says. "People do not always know the difference between a cougar and a bobcat. Or a lynx. Usually, when people say 'mountain lion,' I do not rely on them."

"And you've been walking this road a long time."

"Thirty-six years. But usually I walk only in the dark. Maybe I do not see the mountain lion."

This could be dry humor; in Richard Rohr, the wise Franciscan, I've read that the most common phrase in the Bible is "Be not afraid."

"I should take heart from your example."

"Yes. These animals are shy; they're afraid of everything."

Lights are coming on in the distance, as dusk gives way to darkness; the monk speaks of a Chinese dog he met, the Japanese educational system.

"You know this is not just a hotel with pretty views?" he asks me.

"I know. But I feel there's a longing in many of us, a hunger, for clarity and silence."

"Yes." He gathers his thoughts. "I know a family in Carmel Valley; they have children. When I go to see them, it's a rat race. One coming in here, one coming in there. 'I want to go swimming!' 'I want to go to the basketball game!' 'Please pick me up here, pick me up!' Always this sense of constant agitation.

"Even for us monks, we go to town and when we come back, we speak more loudly, more fast. Everything is a race. People come here and they want to say 'Hail Mary' or 'And with thy spirit!' so fast. We try to slow them down. 'Go and may peace be with you.' A long pause. He looks at me. 'And with thy spirit.'"

Night has fallen around us by now, and he is recalling the General from Italy who could not sleep at night inside his banana-leaf hut in the Camaldolese ashram in India. Because of a bird with a rising call. In the dark, as we stand along the deserted road, the small old monk reproduces the bird's whistle to perfection. He talks of seeing Sai Baba. "There is a power there, definitely. But a Christian would ask, 'Where does the power come from?'"

Then remembering himself, he registers the lights in the distance. "I'm sorry. I met you in daylight, now it is night. But I saw you with this broom and I thought you were going to put it beneath your legs and—whoosh!—right off the edge of the cliff.

"Or maybe you were playing curling."

He prepares to make his way back to the enclosure. "I will see you again. If you do not see me, it means I have met the mountain lion."

6.

How to stay calm amidst the flames? Or trust the dark so deeply that you can walk through it night after night as predators stir on every side? I think of pictures of the Buddha seated, motionless, amidst a circle of fire; faith can't just be "high-premium fire insurance," I've read in a book by a Franciscan. It has to involve submission to an order one can't begin to second-guess.

I think, even more, of the sixty-six-year-old Vietnamese Buddhist monk of my boyhood setting himself on fire in the busy streets of Saigon. Not just to protest his leaders' crackdown on religion, but even more, perhaps, to remind them that death might not be the enemy of life.

One afternoon, at Ree's recommendation, I walk to the very edge of the parking lot outside the retreat-house and then down a narrow, barely paved path, into the ravine that plunges towards the sea. Sidestepping the little wooden sign that says PRIVATE, as Ree had urged, I make my way to the valley floor, where I step into a world of wonders.

There are gremlins here and there among the trees, rocks that look like gateways. Pieces of driftwood with stones in their laps as if to form Nature's own Virgin and Child. Streams made of pebbles, guarded by wind chimes; candles on every side and a Krishna dancing life into creation and extinction on a rock.

"And this our life"—I think of a boyhood exposure to Shakespeare's Forest of Ardennes—"exempt from public haunt, finds tongues in trees, books in the running brooks, sermons in stones, and good in everything."

A FORMER PRIOR had begun to feel that the community could gain from a lay presence, Ree had told me, even a feminine touch. So when a French-Canadian couple, Eric and Thérèse, asked if they could live in the valley next to the monastic enclosure—they could teach young monks to make ceramics that could then be sold in the bookstore—the prior put it to a vote among his brothers and every one of them said yes.

Before long, Thérèse, almost sixty, was shouldering huge boulders to clear ground for a small cottage, while sleeping for the moment in a little trailer lacking even water. In the years that followed, responding to the prior's suggestion, she'd begun to fashion her own sacred space amidst the trees. I see a Buddha, framed by lilies, sporting a turquoise necklace. Lanterns set on branches and next to rocks. Statues and household gods everywhere I turn. The whole wild expanse feels pagan and alive, an alternative church to complement the chapel up the slope.

7.

CHRISTMAS MEANS jammed parking lots and crowded stores: the season of celebration is a torrent of consumption, the time for families to gather is the time when long-forgotten grievances flare up again. Tires shriek in the parking lot, ads on the radio tell us we have to act "NOW." That certainly applies to me: I have to locate an Advent calendar, a Christmas tree, Christmas pudding for my Christmas-loving Hindu mother; she's fretting over Christmas cards, fretting over preparations for our trip next week to the Middle East. I go down to the supermarket in search of eggnog for her, and drivers are riding their horns as they jostle for a single parking space, families are screaming at one another that Uncle Fred is never going to wear that necktie.

. . .

I HAVE TO ESCAPE if only to recall what a holiday means. I pull up at the Hermitage bookstore and the monk on duty breaks into a huge smile.

"How have you all been?"

"Beautiful!" he says. "The sea has been satinate. And the stars! Venus now is so bright it's like the moon. It casts a lunar glow above the water."

"All these years and all these stars, and still you have the capacity to be excited."

"Oh, yes. And this season there are meteorites, too."

He asks me what I've been working on and I mention a novel about faith that has consumed me for months: faith in the midst of confusion and drift.

"It takes a long time to season a monk," he says, looking at me directly. "It's not easy. I've noticed that in Italy, they're more open to other communities than we tend to be. Here some of the younger monks get to be very rigid; they want to hold on to all the pious old ways."

"Why is that, do you think?"

"It's that confusion and drift. This place becomes an anchor for them. But they also need room to grow, to explore. That's the beautiful friction of it."

"This place is a safe house, but it needs to be something else, and more?"

"Exactly."

Learning from Silence

I walk down to the room called Sacred Heart and look out at a sea that is, well, satinate.

Darkness comes early in midwinter, and when I step out of my trailer, into a rounded bowl of stars, Venus, as promised, is making a silver trail across the sea. I start to walk up the slope, then recall whatever was shadowing me near the oak tree all those months ago and turn back round to go inside again.

There's a stick beside the door, surely made for times like this; I see the broom I liked to wield before.

I hear rustling in the undergrowth; something is afoot. I remember the small monk in his black beret, walking each night into the dark.

I head out again, with nothing in my hand, senses on high alert. I can hear more than I can see, and whatever I'm hearing can surely see me better than I see it. For a few steps, a light appears behind me—company—and then it's gone.

I turn and there's nobody in view. I keep on walking down the lonely road even farther from shelter or safety.

"Please enjoy your time in silence," Hiroko had told me before I drove up. "But please don't go out at night. I don't want you to be eaten by a mountain lion!"

Cat's eyes flicker along the road: posts, I assume, to

guide drivers in the dark. I walk to the farthest bench and see the starry rainfall above the thin tracery of the highway. Somewhere I hear the mournful howl of a coyote. The only point of being here, I realize: surrender.

Two hundred miles for a single night, I think next morning, and now two hundred miles back home, after only twenty hours in silence. Was ever any Christmas gift a wiser investment?

8.

"I can't believe you're spending all this time with these old guys in hoods," Steve says one day as we walk beside the sea. His rich sense of comedy is one of his most delightful qualities, but I always sense behind it some hope he's too shy to give full voice to.

"I know." I point out how the sun shines like gunmetal on the water. "I suppose I feel such a sense of promise along this coastline. The New World's great offering to the world. But"—I have to phrase it delicately to a friend from L.A.—"promise can become such a challenge, even an abyss. If you don't have a strong sense of discipline, direction."

Steve looks away, disappointed.

"I just mean that so many worthy causes keep bombarding us with requests. They want more money, new members, they're so keen to seem up-to-the-moment. I like the way these guys almost never ask for anything. They have no interest in being cool. Their longing is to be warm. On fire even."

I remember hearing of a young visitor who came to the Hermitage eager to part with his inheritance of three million dollars. "Don't do it," the monks told him. "Wait till you know what you really want to do with it."

The Buddha's lesson, too: excessive renunciation is still excess.

BACK IN SOPHIA, I break off crusts to feed the jays on the terrace. Just as I never do at home, where the birds are even more abundant. I painstakingly rearrange the little piece of Dove soap wrapper that holds up the unsteady leg on my bathroom sink. As I wash the glass I use for water, I squeeze a little dishwashing liquid in, and register, as never before: one drop of blue and the whole glass is transformed.

WHEN I MAKE my slow way back from the farthest bench in late afternoon, I pass a young woman, legs outstretched at the picnic table beside the road, deep in a book. She'd been there long before, when I'd walked in the other direction, and now she looks up, and I see a face that looks strangely ancient, strong. Straggly dark hair, clothes made for camping.

"Excuse me," she calls out. "Can you tell me what the rule is here?"

"I don't think there's any rule. The monks are just happy if you can savor the quiet. I think the idea is to draw closer to what you love."

"Okay. I can manage that."

Maria comes from Trujillo, in Peru, she tells me, the famous home of writers I bumped through as a teenager. She is one of eight, daughter of a lawyer. All her life she's sensed there must be something more than what we see; a job, a home, a car cannot be the end of the story. She's traveled to Varanasi, to Jerusalem, to the Jokhang Temple in Tibet.

I'm taken aback. "Are you a doctor?"

"Well," she says, looking a little sheepish, "I did get a doctorate in sociology." In French, as it turns out, in Montreal.

"And now . . ."

"Now I'm living in San Francisco. But I want to explore. And I do not have money for a motel. So"—she gestures towards a battered white van—"I thought maybe I could stay on this road. It is safe and quiet here and I am not bothering anybody."

"What is it you're reading?"

She turns over her book, and I see it's the very biography, from more than a decade ago, that I began reading in Hesychia last year.

"I was driving down from Canada," she explains, "and, well . . . I fell in love. We got married. But it didn't last. My whole world collapsed. And that's when I began reading this book. On Wittgenstein. It had such intensity. I really thought, 'My world must have meaning like this!'"

Of course, I think: Wittgenstein actually worked as a gardener in a monastery, living in a toolshed for three months. One of the many ways he tried to humble his dazzling mind and make philosophy a practice rather than mere theory. "I am not a religious man," he wrote, "but I cannot help seeing every problem from a religious point of view."

I look up again, thrilled to engage with the stranger whom in my usual life I'd hurry past.

"Enjoy your stay," I call out as I head back towards my trailer. And then, recalling what I read here, only a year before, "Didn't Wittgenstein say something like, 'The place I really have to get is a place I must already be'?"

BACK IN MY CELL, I start scribbling again; the words keep pouring out. Erotic sketches, long letters, parables. Poems in the style of Emily Dickinson. Notes for myself, postcards, records of memories that come streaming back. Today, for no reason, a Sufi tale, which I transcribe in one transported rush.

Hours later, I can't find it anywhere. I check my notes, every drawer, the suitcase bulging with the pages I've just scrawled. Nothing.

Then at last I see it, in the trash can. Smeared by raspberry yogurt so barely a word is legible on the crumpled paper.

Nothing lasts for long, I think, leaving it where it is; it served its purpose at the time.

Into the Boiler Room

1.

It feels a bit like trespass as I make a hard right just before arriving at the retreat-house, and drive, for the first time ever, past the sign that says, NO ENTRANCE PLEASE. MONASTIC RESIDENCE. For years the monks have been inviting me to come and stay in their midst, especially when all retreatants' rooms are occupied; for years I've said no, greedily clinging to my solitude. Now I want to taste a little of what it is to live—and prepare to die—on the far side of the wall.

I pull up at the rickety, two-story structure known as the Ranch House. Built almost a hundred years ago, it was never meant for monks; it was set up by three men from Wyoming hoping to start a dude ranch here.

Today it looks like Grandpa's neglected folly. TREAD, says a sign on one of the creaking stairs to the second floor, though no one has thought to add "SLOWLY" or

"SOFTLY." My room is even more bare than the ones that retreatants enjoy on the other side of the property. I test the bed, and soft pillows collapse under my negligible weight. I walk down the corridor to the shared toilet, and the seat slips and slides beneath me.

Outside—I pull back fading curtains—I see weeds everywhere, a battered shed, someone carrying a pile of laundry to a shack. Someone else is revving up an ancient car, and someone's driving a golf cart off to take care of the latest drama. The panes on my window are held together with cellophane and hope.

Those on retreat—it comes to me now—get to enjoy silence and light and a heart-lifting expanse of blue sky and blue sea; those on this side of the enclosure have to make do with a scrappy backyard, crowded with bodies pushing wheelbarrows.

IT USED TO BE more austere here, I know: Cabins were built with their backs to the sea so no one would be distracted by the long horizons. Monks were hidden from visitors in the chapel by a barrier, and there were prayers every day at two in the morning, the first of seven daily services. Food was passed to visitors through a cupboard door, and brothers were allowed to receive letters only four times a year.

Finally the General in the motherhouse in Italy who oversees them all felt that this was too much—humanity can so easily get mislaid—and the leash was lightened somewhat so the brothers could live closer to the people that they serve.

But still I feel I'm in some rough and uncared-for, all-male B and B. Not the great seagoing vessel that is my life in the expanse outside; rather, the boiler room behind the scenes where men in blue work clothes are laboring night and day to keep the vessel in motion.

On that side of the wall, I think, we get to speak to God, however we conceive of what's beyond us; on this, the monks find sustenance in caring for one another, looking for the divine in everything around them.

WITH SO LITTLE to divert me in my room—no ocean to look out on here—I head downstairs to explore the "raunchy library," as a monk had described it to me. He wasn't kidding: a couple of books of Woody Allen sketches; the impenitently love-soaked novels of Isaac Bashevis Singer and Graham Greene; science fiction and cop thrillers. Everything that doesn't quite fit in the monks' capacious library across the way.

Also, a "World Class" 160-gram Frisbee; a telescope; an exercise bike.

One of the books on most prominent display is the memoir of the Hollywood producer who went through seven wives, *The Kid Stays in the Picture*; as I carry it up to my room, I almost walk into a worker who's doing pull-ups off the rafters of the building, so vigorously I fear he'll bring the whole place down.

I HEAD INTO the vast refectory kitchen, and find one of the most outgoing of the brothers fretting over pots and pans. "This bloody peeling of onions," he exclaims, with a large, infectious smile. "It never stops!"

"It must be a good break from what you usually do."

He looks up, surprised. "It's the inner onion I'm talking about." A joyful laugh. "The invisible stuff!"

Then, noting my uncertainty: "Please, whatever you feel like doing, just do it. Because if you're feeling stifled, if you're worrying about what you should or shouldn't do, then the whole thing's lost.

"Don't worry about whether it is or isn't right to get some food from here and take it back to your cell. Two or three of the guys do that every night. Don't think of right and wrong here; everything's right."

AS I WALK OUT, I hear a small throng of voices in the chapel, singing, "Alleluia." I head off into the public area and the birds, the sea, the clouds seem to be singing the same thing.

SOME ROOMS IN the Ranch House have pillows, some have glasses, mugs; mine, for no reason I can discern, sports a refrigerator. The rooms themselves might be old monks, each eccentric in his own way, each having gathered different worn supplies over forty years of living very close to the bone.

SUCH A FRESH, unpretentious circle of souls, I think, as I start to chat with the brothers, meal after meal. Yet all pointed upwards, like tipped arrows. Bright, sociable, kind—teasing one another about their feast days—as they fashion a makeshift community in the middle of the wilderness.

One of them, whose 240-watt smile goes with the warm poise and confidence of a CEO, is saying "Omigod" when I meet him, words drowned out by a low-flying plane.

"We're fighting to preserve our silence," he explains, radiant in his white Nike T-shirt. He's just been quoted on the subject in a local newspaper, he tells me—above, as he reports with a mischievous gleam, Robert Redford.

"The Navy is bombing both monks and condors!"

I'm munching on pizza, left over from the fiftieth

wedding party of the couple who live in the canyon, and he tells me about the Catholic Hindu monk who dressed in a dhoti and ate with his hands while sleeping every night on the floor of the Camaldolese ashram in southern India.

Bede Griffiths was so deeply rooted in his Christian faith that he knew he could retrieve the "other half of his soul" by steeping himself in a very different tradition. On the floor of the Benedictine ashram where he lived, Shantivanam—the Forest of Peace—are written the liberating words: "We are here to awaken from the illusion of our separateness."

I never forget meeting the man outside the bookstore the first year I arrived, with his long white beard and melodious Tennysonian voice, speaking of the universal call to contemplation, his long walks as a boy through golden summer evenings in England.

"It was as if everything that took him East just broke, broke through," the monk now tells me, of the stroke Bede Griffiths suffered three years before his death. "The whole feminine thing: Mary, something in the right brain. He said it was as if somebody hit him on the left side of his brain and it went right through."

"I was just reading how the word *blessing* comes from the French *blessure*. The word for 'wound.'"

"Yes. That makes sense. A blessing can go right through you like a wound."

"But a wound can be a blessing, too."

He laughs, as if to say, "You've got me."

IN THE KITCHEN, a monk is pulling down one small bottle after another, scattering spices across the communal meal he's preparing. "I always get up early when it's my turn to cook," he says. "To think about color, think about texture."

"I hadn't realized meals were so important."

"It's a hard life." He looks straight at me. "The guys need something to brighten their day."

THE TWO DOGS in the cloister are Buddy and Scooter; the gray tabby cat in whom they once took an unholy interest is Elizabeth. Father Robert brought her into his cell to protect her; on the back of the book he published about a year in the life of a prior, *Love on the Mountain*, he's pictured snuggling with his long-haired friend.

Robert was the community's barber long before he became its prior; his spiritual director, he wrote, was a wife and mother, who offered him wisdom he might never have received in an all-male community. I watch him and his old friends go about their days, and I think of Merton writing to Henry Miller that an individual can be a zero.

Nothing in himself, but put him next to anything, and its value increases by a factor of ten.

THAT NIGHT I'm shocked awake in the dark hours; someone is walking up and down the corridor. I had thought the whole house unoccupied save for myself. Now I hear footsteps treading past my door and then disappearing; no creak on the stairs to suggest a departure.

"The Ranch House is older than the monastery," I say at lunch to an elderly monk. "It's seen a lot."

"Just rats and mice," he replies. "I'm sure it wasn't anything."

SLOWLY I BEGIN TO PATTERN out a routine, as if to make the enclosure home. In the mornings, I sit and write in my bare space, then take a long walk in the expansive retreatants' area, high above the sea. In the sleepy afternoons, I go to the monks' library and browse through Northrop Frye, Henry Miller, shelves and shelves of Zen and Sufism. There are lavish books of photography on hand, two or three aisles of poetry. Walker Percy, Evelyn Waugh, Bruce Chatwin. A globe for the monks to revolve.

In the evenings, I head into the huge freezer to browse among leftover pieces of pizza and salmon; the kitchen might be the galley on a ship, filled with oversized spoons and implements, shelves of supplies, the bowl brought out on Sundays piled high with KitKats and bars of Twix. As I emerge from the storage area one night, I glimpse a monk, returned late from some duty in the world, eating quickly at a counter, like a mouse.

"Who are you?" he asks. I don't know what to say.

THE SUN, I begin to see, is just as strong here as on the other side of the wall; it simply happens to fall on a vegetable garden and old chairs, a tin bucket for a trash can, someone's toothbrush in the sink. My days among the monks actually warm me more than what I experience in the retreatants' world; they're more convivial, enveloping. I do dishes, return to my bare room (St. Paul the Hermit), see a burly, bearded monk arrange lilies in a slender silver vase to place inside the chapel.

THE TALK AT LUNCH IS WEATHER, a trip to Monterey, the news (more scandals in the Church), the preached retreat entitled "Becoming Fire." There are two recluses in residence, and the job of one is to tend to the other, who's lost his sight; the sighted one cuts up his brother's food for him, changes his clothes. "And he's what we in Massachusetts call 'brash,'" says one of the monks beside me. "Which means loud, cranky, all over the place. So the two of them just bicker like an old couple. 'Eat this!' 'No, I'm not going to. . . .'"

The old man I met along the road, in his beret, spots a new face in the refectory and comes to sit down next to me. "Everything you see in life," he says, between quick, birdlike bites, "you see in a monastery. You see someone killed in a monastery. In Naples we have a church and someone asked if he could get married there, and the prior said no. It's the Camaldolese way to stay away from crowds. So the man and his friends beat the prior up. So bad, he had to go to the hospital!"

Another tells me of the helium balloons the monks filled for Eric and Thérèse on their fiftieth wedding anniversary, the delighted smiles on the couple's faces upon being surprised by a party of white-cowled friends.

Returning to my room, I hear "Pico" across the courtyard and see the worker, somewhat bedraggled, who's been here for as long as I remember.

"You recall that time we met along the road?" I ask him. "Talking about *Holy the Firm*?"

"I do," he says, grinning. "I can't remember what I did yesterday, but I do remember that. I suppose memory is more discerning than consciousness."

"You're a scholar, by the sound of it?"

"Oh, no. I'm just in maintenance. Plumbing and such. It's not very glamorous, but customer satisfaction, when I fix the toilets for the monks, is pretty high."

"How are you today, Pico?" the prior had asked me at lunch.

"Well. Too well."

"Don't worry," he said, smiling broadly. "We can fix that."

When I drive back towards home, onto the now empty highway, I'm biting my lip to stay clearheaded. The monks have been telling me about the "gift of tears," which speaks for the grace of feeling for one's neighbors. The last time I'd passed the worker doing his chin-ups on the rafters, I'd seen a book splayed out beside him. *An Invitation to Love*.

2.

ONE HOT SUMMER day I drive down again to visit my droll Zen friend from the mountain behind Los Angeles. As I turn onto the quiet residential street on which he lives, in a broken part of the city, it's to find him seated on the curb, in the blistering July heat, in suit and tie.

A computer lies in the gutter at his feet.

"Yesterday's drama," he explains with a small smile.

He leads me past the house into the back garden and up some stairs to where he maintains a homemade recording studio; part of his practice, I imagine, involves making no distinction between what's inside the meditation hall and what's not.

A tall young woman with a rush of dark hair under her straw hat stands up and lights a stick of incense, then proceeds to fashion high-voice curlicues around the taped melody that comes thumping out. My friend, always courtly, ushers me into a chair beside him, and starts telling me about his trips to India to hear a retired bank executive talk about the dissolution of all boundaries.

In Zen he'd lived that truth out, and felt the pain that can't be argued away; in Mumbai the polished Indian metaphysician had given him a universal framework for what he'd felt.

We take a simple lunch around a table—he, his partner in life and art, his daughter with her camera—and then he invites me out into the patch of grass on the front lawn, facing the street.

I sit down on the folding chair he's brought with us, and gaze at the flowers; no word from the figure at my side.

I sit there longer. Nothing to join us but the sunlight and the words we're not speaking.

Finally—maybe twenty minutes have passed—I think the unbroken silence might be a hint. "I should be going," I say, pushing back my chair. "You have things to do."

My host looks up at me, beseeching. "Please don't go."

THE RECORD HE'S brought out since our last meeting—*Ten New Songs*—could have been called *Songs from a Cell*. All I hear, when I listen to it, is his bare cabin on the dark and lonely mountain where I first met him. Sitting through the night till birds announce the morning.

Amidst all that passes through his mind in the monastery—the memories of making love, the people he'll never see again, the life that's slipping away—is what can seem the hardest truth of all: his life in robes has shown him how much he belongs to what he's taken to calling "Boogie Street."

There are gifts you can't return, he sings, and his gift may be for communicating to and in the world; it's as if the very vows he took when becoming a monk have brought him back to the unexalted heart of L.A.

CONTEMPLATION ISN'T A CURE for anxiety, the wise and uplifting Benedictine Father Thomas Keating says; it just lets you look at life a little differently. The dark places don't go away when you step into silence; if anything, they rise to the surface. But here you can see them clearly as you never could when barreling along the freeway.

Look at the suffering you're causing, too, in yourself and others—always more important than the suffering you're enduring. It's hard to curse anyone in this clement light, I realize, in part because I'm not locked inside my own perspective. I write as many letters as I can while I'm above the sea, because this is the one place where, as my Buddhist friends say, the mind is as vast as the blue open sky.

"You must have had that quality inside you all along," says a sympathetic friend.

"Inside all of us, I think." None of this is particular to me.

BY NOW THERE'S a younger presence living on the property, to help the monks: a tall, slim woman with the calm face and clear heart of a nun, who lives in a small space beside the bookstore and, like the male workers in the enclosure, helps clean the rooms and tend to retreatants' needs. I enter my cell and her touch is everywhere: the flower left in a shapely vase as thin as a tiny bottle of wine, the calligraphed greeting on a laminated card. I ask her a question—about prayer or about soup—and every time I come away with a pure, true answer.

I take a walk with her one night, all the way down to the bottom of the hill, and I hear of my new friend's life in other spiritual communities, run, as often as not, according to a single man's dictates. Here there's a prior, but the feeling always is of some higher authority, something impersonal and centuries old, refined over generations.

"I wonder if it helps to have a system to rail against more than just one man?" I say.

We keep walking down to where the moon silvers the ocean.

Learning from Silence

. . .

SOMETIMES I WONDER—and friends keep asking—how spending all this time in silence has changed me. I can hardly count the ways, now that joy seems the opposite of pleasure and freedom arises out of an embrace of limits; it's impossible to take so seriously the self that huffs and puffs along the highway. When I find myself in a crowded airport terminal, I'm drawn, as if magnetically now, to a quiet corner in the sun; as I wait for Hiroko to come back from work—will it be twenty minutes or ninety?—I turn off the lights and listen to Bach.

Some nights, of course, I still wake up in the dark, unable to sleep. I worry about that cough nearby, fear for Hiroko if I should go before she does. Chaos and suffering seem endless.

Then I recall the sun burning on the water far below and feel part of something larger in which nothing is absolute or final.

THE NEXT TIME I drive up the narrow path—the monks seem to be beckoning me ever closer—I'm given an actual monastic cell in which to stay, a large, empty modern space with a kitchen, a garden, an old-fashioned stove in the middle of the room. On the wall, a delicate Kuan Yin, Chinese goddess of compassion. At the entrance, a framed statement from St. Benedict saying, in effect, that any guest is welcome for so long as he might wish to stay. Should he indulge in "gossip or contumacious behavior," however, he will be taken in hand by "two stout monks" and led out of the enclosure.

Benedict did not insist on austerities; he allowed wine in the monastery, two cooked vegetables every day. But in his "schools of love," he seemed to consider "murmuring" the most dangerous poison of all.

THERE ARE NO LOCKS on the doors within the enclosure—all the rooms seem to be hexagonal—and few locks on the conversation. At lunch I hear how the cells in the motherhouse, in Italy, are shaped, each one, like a nautilus; how Romuald wished that each monastery be home to just seven monks. Seven bells a day, says a monk beside me, would be just perfect, instead of the thirty they have now. One tells me about seeing the new Harry Potter movie ("Well, I was leading a retreat down in L.A."); another about how he's getting to use the frequent-flier miles from the monastery's credit card to head down to Rio. "We have a house in Brazil," he explains, "and I saw the other six continents while I was cooking for the Coast Guard. Now I can see the seventh and end my travels."

One, perhaps remembering the warnings up in the

retreat-house, reminds me that the first miracle of St. Jerome, according to legend, was to rescue a lion with a thorn in its paw.

To which another replies, with brio, "If you do spot a mountain lion, make sure you don't look like a deer!"

"Some people find us a bit boisterous," a monk apologizes to me as the meal draws to a close, to which the prior adds, "I hope you're not going to find us a distraction."

Two days later, I plan to escape to Big Sur for an afternoon: I can browse in the Henry Miller Memorial Library, "Where Nothing Happens," as the sign says, sit in the sun in my favorite café, just below the restaurant named for the drug in Homer that makes all cares disappear. I can look in on the little inn with no telephones or keys. At lunch in the refectory, just as I'm preparing to head off, a monk confesses, "I've swallowed three flies this year. That's a record." Where else will I find anything so unexpected, I think, and cancel the trip I don't need to take.

This is the recipe for happiness, I read in a novel by David Grossman. "Believe in the eternal thing in yourself, and do not aspire to it."

. . .

My last day in the enclosure, at lunch, I find myself next to the older woman who's been living on the property for as long as I've been coming, more than twenty years now. We've never spoken before, but it's hard to miss the playful sparkle with which she observes the world around her.

"How are you?" I ask.

"I am well enough. You know I am the oldest person on this mountain?"

"Really?"

"Eighty-seven. And last year a tornado came and blew down seven of my trees." Thérèse sips at her water. "You have to take care of beauty, to make the most of it, because so soon it is gone."

Two years ago, she continues, her husband died, his heart giving out during a sudden fire evacuation. "So that gave me the blessing of great silence and solitude. And silence, it is the greatest blessing. When you are old, devotions, rituals, icons, they fall away; you go straight to the heart."

Her eyes are red, but there's no hesitation in her voice.

"Of course, spirituality is horizontal, not just vertical. You have to be with other human beings; it's not about just getting things for yourself. But you come to see that when things are taken away from you, it is to make room for higher purp—no, higher understanding."

"As with your trees?"

"Exactly! It gives you more room to see. When I woke up and found the storm had taken away two sycamores, I thought, 'My friends!' But now I have a wider view. It is much better."

3.

MY MONK FRIEND LEONARD is standing at the door, as ever, outside his modest home when I pull up. He's come down from the monastery, but a monk's discipline and attentiveness—a monk's readiness to serve—seem never to have left him.

Almost as soon as I enter his simple room, he asks me, as on every visit, whether I'm married. I am, I say, as always, and he shakes his head. "That's the real training. Sitting on top of a mountain in a meditation hall is easy by comparison."

It's not, I know; I've watched him go through most of seven days and seven nights in meditation. But he understands me perfectly when I explain, "It was only being alone that gave me the courage to get married."

Learning from Silence

. . .

As darkness falls, he leads me out to his car and drives us towards a taverna not far away; impatient Angelenos, riding their horns, give him the finger as they accelerate past.

"Hurrying home to light the candles," he observes.

Before he became a monk, his songs were thick with religion: he was constantly referring to Jesus or St. Paul, crosscutting Old Testament allusions with Buddhist riddles. As soon as he took on robes, the verses began to deal with oblivion, with letting go of everything he loves, not least those inspiring parables. When he sings about "going home," it's clear he's addressing the place most of us try not to think about.

On Chanukah, I join him and his family for Shabbat—he faithfully observes the rites of his native Judaism even after becoming a Zen monk—and he tells me, shaken, how a friend he had trusted for decades made off with just about all his money while he was up on the mountain.

"Maybe that's one reason you had to be up on the mountain."

He smiles. It's really his son and daughter and their children that he worries about; after they come in to help wash the dishes, everyone joins in on a chorus of "What Shall We Do with the Drunken Sailor?"

As I prepare to leave, I think of all he's given me. "Did you ever read Etty Hillesum?"

"I don't believe I've had the privilege."

I tell him about the young Dutch woman who, as the Nazis drew closer, rose out of what seemed a typically confused life to an astonishing wisdom and confidence that a saint might envy.

"It's something she says. 'Kneeling can be more intimate than sex.'"

WHY DID I SUDDENLY THINK of Hillesum? Maybe, I reflect, as I make my slow way home through traffic, because it's always been Leonard's central concern: how to live with the suffering that every day (and every night) throws up. Desire has so often gotten him into deepest trouble; letting go of his will, his wishes, is perhaps the truest way to peace.

I think of Hillesum, in her midtwenties, in Amsterdam in the 1930s, in love with her palm-reading psychoanalyst, in love with an even older widower in whose house she lives, unsure of herself and of her destiny. Then the net of oppression begins to close around her and she starts to grow more and more radiant in her selflessness and certainty.

She volunteers to serve in the dark and muddy transit camp called Westerbork, and to serve, moreover, in the hospital; around her is an orphanage, a mortuary and "a madhouse being built." She's condemned to sleep on metal springs—no mattress or blanket in the freezing winter—and to scrounge for food; she's squeezed into a room that's six foot by nine, surrounded by the dying. Her life, she writes in the midst of this squalor, is "one long sequence of inner miracles."

She steadfastly remains the opposite of a Pollyanna: "you can't play the ostrich here." Every Monday a train rolls into the bleak settlement and every Tuesday it pulls out, carrying a thousand or more to Auschwitz. "Several suicides last night," she writes to a friend, of those about to be taken away, "with razors and so on." Life would be bleak, she confesses, "if you don't have the inner strength while you are here to understand that all outer appearances are simply a passing show, as nothing besides the great inner splendor (I can't think of a better word right now) inside us."

MONKS HAVE CONSECRATED their lives to this assumption, but how many are asked to put it to the test as she was? She could, in fact, return to Amsterdam quite often if she chose; friends repeatedly offer her ways of making an escape and staying in a safe house. She refuses them all, as if her only purpose now is to tend to the condemned.

When gallstones force her to visit a doctor, he's furious, she reports, that she is beaming: it's only her body that's afflicted, she explains, not her heart or spirit.

It confounds me how this typical-sounding young soul can summon such clarity and conviction. She grows impatient when others speak of "making the most of things" or "seeing the good in everything." Life, she knows, is all we have to work with. But like the most enlightened beings, she seems to see light wherever she looks. She seeks out the yellow lupines on the bleak heath. She watches priests go about their prayers, as unconcerned as she. An old man she knows points at the villas where the camp's administrators live and says, "*They* are the ones who live behind barbed wire."

I can never read her story without giving up all my simple ideas of what sacrifice means, or justice. In September 1943 she and her parents and brother are finally loaded on the train for the three-day trip to Poland; her parents are gassed upon arrival. Her death, at twenty-nine, is reported two months later. A few days after her train passes out of Westerbork, farmers find a postcard she threw out of the window as she was being taken to her death. "We left the camp singing," she confesses.

4.

How to prepare for death? It becomes a central question in any monastery, and one without an answer. I spend time with monks and nuns, I realize, because they're giving themselves full-time to the essential practices: learning how to love in the midst of loss. And how to hope in the face of death. But the nature of their lives—new fires surge above the chapel, and the earth begins to crack beneath their feet (the monks of Big Sur are living on a major fault line)—allows few certainties. The most devout of monks, the wisest light in one community I know, suddenly, as he's nearing the end, turns to the bottle; a professor of political science who's a friend, and cheerfully admits to no religious practice, sits calmly in his bed watching the news and chatting with me and Hiroko a week or so before he knows he'll be gone.

In the journal he published of a year as prior, Father

Robert keeps coming back to this: at one point, a doctor finds a growth in his armpit and dryly reports that the possibility of its being benign is either zero or a hundred percent. The generally cheerful prior admits to "waves of panic" as he drives back to the monastery; he recalls his brother, who died from such a growth after months and months of treatment, his hair gone, his features "practically unrecognizable."

When the news comes in that he's okay, Robert writes that he's been through a "good fire drill." But it's not exactly a reprieve, he knows, only a postponement. He can't say that God has spared him, since none of us gets spared in the end.

ALL AROUND ME in the hills of Big Sur, regular folks are facing down this riddle in their own ways, freed from inessentials and often with a keener sense of community than of faith. I drive up the steep, narrow path across from Highway 1, barely thirty minutes north of the monastery, punch in a code and watch the gates swing back. Then, for ten or fifteen minutes, I jolt up barely paved roads, through a grove of redwoods, to where dozens of people are living as simply as they can, off the grid at times, sometimes an hour or more from the nearest paved road.

Finally I pull up at an octagonal glass tepee: inside, my

young friend Sam is seated on the ground, works of fiction and reportage lining the floor around him and a bed on one side, suspended in midair. He reads, he writes, he offers shelter to friends whose work in the emergency room is consuming them; when fires break out across the state, he hurries off to help, since he has training and experience.

Just as often, the blaze is right here, and he cooks dinner for the firefighters, offers them a place to crash; none of them is deterred by the fact that his outhouse is down a slope and, when I look in, so teeming with flies, I cannot enter.

Along the way is Henry Miller's house, still on the edge of its cliff; just here, Miller imagined a "God-filled community . . . even if none of its members believed in [a] God." Nearby, a home built more or less underground by the area's famous architect, with a banana tree flowering in the living room and a shower next to the rock face. The doors of the small structure are shaped to resemble gateways to a sacred space; a small oval window is positioned so that, during the winter solstice, the sun rises and sets at its center. Furnishings are mostly a monk's simple sink and a long desk.

Often, I hear, the entrance road is completely washed away by rain, and supplies have to be helicoptered in. The citizens of Partington Ridge exchange such things as they collect, much as they place book drops around the wilderness. "I wonder if this is the future of monasticism," I say to Sam. "People living close to the elements and together, but not bound by a single doctrine."

Then he drives me up to the top of the mountain, where a tall young artist is putting the finishing touches on a life-size sculpture of a "Black Watcher." These spooky presences—ten feet high, jet-black, with wide-brimmed hats—are said to stand sentinel all across the Big Sur hills. "The Indians saw them, the early Spaniards saw them. I don't know," says the sculptor. "Maybe they're just trees. Every place has got to have its spirits."

Light or dark, it's hard to tell. His last piece was an installation in which he dug a very deep grave and invited visitors to step inside.

WHEN I HEAR THE RAP on the pillar at the edge of my deck, I know it's the warm monk to whom I've grown so close. In his hand is his mug, two tea bags and a box of Walkers shortbread. We sit in comfort in the sunlight, a pot of tea between us, and he tells me how he knew, when he was eight years old, that this should be his life. He'd served in the army briefly—not a bad preparation—and then he'd ended up on what he calls "the apostolic path," taking his teachings from door to door, sometimes listening to confessions for six hours at a stretch.

Yet all along something deeper was calling him to solitude.

"My two biggest problems here," he says right out, "are the problem with leisure and the problem with loneliness. I'm a type A personality. I'm used to doing things all the time. It can be hard just to sit still and do nothing."

"Don't they say that acedia, the noonday demon, is the monk's biggest threat?"

"That's right! And with loneliness there are several different levels. The Catholic Church has always told us that the body is ugly. That the spirit wants to escape from the body. And if you ask me, that—pardon the expression—is bullshit. You can't just wipe out the body. I used to see these guys who'd been raised in the old system, and they'd never had a human touch. Something in them was dead."

His smile shines electric in his tanned face. "Some days I go barefoot in my cell. I need to feel the ground underneath my feet. Sometimes, if it's nice, I'll bar my door and take off all my clothes!"

His form of worship, he says, is waking up at 4:10 with a cup of tea. Sometimes to see the morning star, sometimes the day come to life. "And at night I like to pour myself a nice glass of wine and read a novel.

"Romuald deliberately softened the Rule. He built his monasteries in the mountains, among the poor. At a time when most monasteries were great centers of power. He always stressed they should be simple, unadorned.

"Really, I just want to commune with God, which is myself by another name. Loneliness is about the journey towards the self. Some of the guys come here to run away. From something in their past, from their own sexuality. And what they find is that they come right up against that in the silence."

I think of myself, so lonely, even terrified, on the nights when the heavens bring storms. For me, it's just a day or two, alone in the desert; for him, it's the life he's promised himself to, of what St. Benedict called "single combat in the wilderness."

5.

IN ALL MY SEASONS HERE I've met only one affliction: on very hot days, at exactly this altitude, the flies start to congregate. They cluster round my eyes, my ears; they hover perpetually at the edge of consciousness. I sit on a bench, to look out across the sea, and soon my hands are flapping and swatting convulsively. I long for fog, so they'll disperse, then wonder how I can be hoping for an end to summer radiance.

In the bookstore, they buzz around the placid, smiling monk on duty, undeterred by the netting at the entrance designed to keep them out. On the terrace outside, the ears of a cat are twitching unstoppably. I head back to my trailer, and find that one has gotten into the room, then another. I'd like to open the door to let them out, but who knows how many more might then come in?

I lie on my bed, but still I can't forget them; I hunger to

go out, to enjoy the beauty of the day, but they're what await me outside. They're buzzing at the screen behind my window, as if eager to get out; I wonder if I should try to thwack them towards an early death or run the risk of pulling the screen back.

A monk on the road today is wearing a kind of screen over his face, to keep them off; others see them as a trial they can't afford to dodge. I know only that I'm not here, when they are, but I'm nowhere else; I'm in that part of myself I come here expressly to leave behind.

FINALLY, I FORCE MYSELF OUT: these are days I can never regret, and if I miss my chance to enjoy them, I'll never forgive myself. As I begin walking down the road, a new worker comes past, excited. His white beard and glasses make him look like a monk with cowboyish intentions.

"You know that oak tree by the picnic tables?" He's almost breathless. "Well, the sun was just coming up over the hill. And when it did, the rays began to stream through the tree, and I saw these cobwebs everywhere. And some of them were broken, or messed up, but others were shining, huge, from the branches."

He shakes his head, at a brief loss for words. "You think you've seen everything. After you've been here a few days, you say, 'Nothing can surprise me now.' But then, every day, something happens, and you just go, 'Wow!' There's always something new to make me catch my breath."

IN MY CELL, by the light of my table lamp—my face reflected back to me in the window as if it were hers—I page, very slowly, through the huge book of poems left behind by Emily Dickinson. She chose to live in her own enclosure, more hermit than any monk might be, and dared to look again and again at the final transport: "'Twas just this time last year, I died." Everything looks different in the eye of Eternity, she knew, and every distinction fades with oblivion; her great thought experiment was to survey the world around her as if she were posthumous.

Dressed in the white of a shroud, watching the men and women she loved walk into the distance down below, she never tried to look away from the ultimate facts of life. I shiver as I sit before her presentiments—"It's coming—the postponeless creature"—and recall how even in her teens, in a cheery Valentine's Day poem—"Oh the Earth was made for lovers"—she couldn't resist reminding us that "The *worm* doth woo the *mortal*, death claims the living bride."

6.

I'M SITTING IN A LITTLE hotel in Bogotá when a message flashes from my Hindu nun friend in California: the Hermitage is encircled by fire, yet again. All the TV channels are showing pictures of the cluster of cabins alone among the flames. Who can resist the parable of fifteen men in white hoods praying, in their remote home in the wilderness, while "acts of God" rewrite the land around them?

THREE DAYS LATER I fly back to Santa Barbara and when I come out from the small terminal, it's to be greeted not by my mother, as I expect, but by a friend; he tells me I don't have a home to return to, pointing to where rivers of orange are crisscrossing the dark hills.

A hundred neighbors are taking shelter in the high

school down the road, sleeping in the cafeteria or the gym, as he takes me to the same place where I slept after our previous house burned down. Pets are being kept in crates on tennis courts. Everyone is being asked to unplug plasma TVs; firefighters are being treated—yet again—for smoke inhalation.

Next day, the headline on the front page of the local paper, just below the photo of a masked sheriff's deputy diverting traffic at the foot of our road, describes further unsettledness two hundred miles to the north: "Wildfire closes in on Big Sur retreats."

WHERE TO GO and what to do? When I step out of our temporary quarters, at first light, I don't know whether to look up to the hills, where the sun is black and smoke shrouds exactly the place where our rebuilt home ought to be. Or to look away, lest I see all that's missing. Almost by reflex, I try to fill the empty hours by driving up to the local Benedictine monastery I've discovered nearby, in the mountains. Parking my car in its silence, I walk down to sit within its sunlit garden. The ocean in the distance, the haze on the far side of town.

Twenty aircraft are dropping fire retardant on the flames that roar towards our house; a DC-10 has been flown in to intensify the battle. Firefighters are coming in from everywhere, but many are needed for the 333 other active wildfires across the state; maps online show where the blaze will go next, starting with our home.

At dinner that night an old friend asks, more or less casually, "Are you going home tonight?"

I look over to where the sky is black: "I don't think I have a home to go back to."

FOR NIGHT AFTER NIGHT, I dream of fire and then one morning I awaken to the news that our house is safe, for now, and so is the Hermitage. Before the year is through, however, the next fire takes down the monastery where I went—my local refuge—and all its monks' possessions.

THE SACRED IS not a sanctuary, I'm moved to remember; it's a force field. In many ways a forest fire. You can try controlled burns or back burning, you can walk towards the heat, but its power comes from the fact that it can't begin to be controlled, or anticipated.

I recall stopping off at a cave along the Mekong River, a few hours from the Laotian city of temples, Luang Prabang. Some tall attendant deities were standing there, almost Egyptian in their shape and posture.

I stood beside them transfixed: this was not the Buddha

sitting in serene meditation. These figures were feminine, upright, sturdy; they looked ready to take off on a long march.

"We should go," said Hiroko, coming back to where I stood.

"Just another minute."

She headed out. Minutes passed. She came back. "The man is saying it's time to go."

"I know. Just a few minutes more."

Finally, she came and dragged me out by the arm. "What is it?" she said, as we came out into the daylight.

"I have to go back."

"It's time to leave."

"Just for a few minutes."

This time she came in with me, and recited the Heart Sutra in front of the statues, convinced that something in them was trying to carry me away. We weren't surprised, hours later, to hear that many people had taken shelter in these caves during the bombing of the Vietnam War, never to emerge again.

SIX MONTHS ON, it was her chance to feel possessed. We were in a church in Florence, and she hurried out, breathing fast.

"What is it?" We sat along a bench in the sun.

"It's like a stone on my chest. I can't breathe."

"What is?"

"The blood everywhere on the cross. The dead bodies. The feet of that man. Inside the black cloth, whispering."

For me, born to the tradition, it was mere background noise; for her, it had lost none of its primal charge and power.

YET STILL I come back to the little cluster of huts upon the hillside. It offers no protection against the facts of life, or death. It seems ready to be wiped out—or cut off from the world again—at any moment. Yet something in the silence seems to outlast our little lives and hopes. Not just in the immemorial rocks and sea and trees, but in its presentation of a world in which the mortal self disappears.

It's not—ever—a world of loss. Rather, one of release, a freedom from the ways we deface the silence.

"IT IS SURPRISING"—I remember the words from Admiral Byrd I read on one of my first visits—"approaching the final enlightenment, how little one really has to know or feel sure about."

BACK IN THEIR EMBATTLED HOME, the monks pick up their lives as ever once they return, heading to the chapel

Learning from Silence

four times a day, preparing their fruitcake in a World War II–era military supply pizza oven. "It's like marriage," I remember one monk telling me of his commitment. But marriage, I think, to someone you can never hold or even see. Marriage to a presence that's impossible to grasp and leaves you alone with a heart that's dangerously easy to doubt.

Now the monk on duty in the bookstore asks me where I've been, and I tell him of my latest assignments: exotic tales of Ladakh and Easter Island can be a gift, perhaps, to someone living in a cluster of huts a long way from the nearest gas station.

"I'm lucky," I confess. "My job takes me to many places. And I've been saving up to take my mother to the Holy Land."

"You see a lot," he says.

"I suppose so. But somehow"—how to say this in a way that doesn't sound ungrateful or entitled?—"it feels like looking at the beautiful wrapping on a present. The real treasure is what's inside the box." I gaze around us at the nine hundred acres, silent in the sunlight.

ONE HOT BLUE SPRING afternoon—Passion Sunday, as I've heard it called—I labor up the dusty path, past the broken sheds, past the workers' shacks, past rows of cardboard trash, past boxes of Iams cat food, up to a lake that now looks wan and dry: no rainfall this California winter. At the top, lupines, purple and white, begin to carpet the meadow. Ticks everywhere. Snakes doze along the path.

Following a trail across the empty meadow, I come to a homemade wall, like something from Druid England. It's in the shape of an L, as if to offer protection.

"A man came to us," a monk explains next day at lunch, "he was thirty-nine and he had been through the most terrible life. His life was all hurt. His father disappeared before he was born, his mother married someone else and had some other children; she passed him along to someone else, he joined his father in the diplomatic service. He was bumped along from place to place. You could tell that: quick, very sharp, but he never let anyone in.

"And I told him, 'I'm sorry. We can't give you what you need. We can't help you in your brokenness. But stay here for a bit. Go and rest in the fields. Take off your shirt and enjoy the sun.' And about a month later, he asked if he could take me up to the lake, and what you saw is what he'd been doing.

"I asked him, 'Which is your mother?' and he pointed to this big rock, huge. Another was when he was cast out by her. Every stone corresponded to something he'd been through. And out of it he made this piece of art. He told me, 'Now I've done this, I can go on.'

"I burst into tears."

Learning from Silence

I hold my tongue because the monk seems close to tears again.

WHEN NEXT I PULL UP to the bookstore to check in, there's a woman, unusually, seated at the high stool beside a small table on the outside terrace, not far from the sign on the side door reminding everyone of the weekly AA meeting on Friday night, "Fire on the Mountain."

I walk past, and then something moves me to look over. "Maria!" It was years ago that we'd met at the picnic table and I hadn't expected the seeker and sociologist from Peru to be camping here again.

She looks up from her book and smiles.

"What are you reading this time?"

She turns over the book, and I see the same cover I know well: the biography of Wittgenstein. "I'm reading it again," she explains. "It seems to fit the place."

It does. So much of the man's rich search had to do with asking how much of "what is good is also divine."

Besides, I can never get over the fact that one of the brilliant minds of the century chose to walk away from his fellowship at Cambridge to teach in obscure village schools around Austria, where locals mocked him for his wealth. He led his young students on stargazing expeditions; he listed his profession in the Vienna digest as "architect." Born to one of the richest families in the land, he gave away most of his money and volunteered to serve on the front in World War I. Sometimes, he found himself carrying bombs along an unsteady plank and later he worked in a hospital.

"It's strange," I say. "We quote him all the time, and people are always talking about his books. But maybe it's his silences, his disappearances, that really affect us in the end?"

Into the Mystery

1.

To celebrate the one thousandth birthday of the Camaldolese congregation, the monks organize a gathering, at a retreat-house by the sea ninety minutes to the north of their home. Friends converge from every direction. A hundred and fifty of us in all, from Asia and Europe, from Santa Fe and upstate New York; Christian and Buddhist and nothing at all. Suddenly what has always been such a deliciously solitary experience for me unfolds within a jam-packed hall; the emblem for the order, I'm reminded, draws from the ancient image of two peacocks drinking from a common chalice.

One monk stands before us and tells us the history of the Camaldolese: a century ago, he says, its numbers dwindled to just thirty, but still the fire refused to go out. The prior in his talk explains that to "sit in your cell as in paradise" really means to "sit in your self as in paradise."

A monk from Italy, the Visitator here to check up (as he does every three years) on his Californian brothers, points out how "people need the silence to hear themselves."

Then comes personal testimony, and we pass across a deeper threshold. "My partner was dying of liver cancer," a man says, fighting back emotion, "and at one point she just said out loud, 'Stop looking after me! You need to look after yourself. Go to the Hermitage.'"

A tall, elegant gentleman, informally but impeccably dressed, deep tan setting off his trim mustache and gray hair, recalls, "I first came to the Camaldolese monastery in 1996. And I didn't like it. But I loved it. And the tension between the two is what makes me keep coming. There is much about Christianity I don't like, and much about contemporary Christians I *really* don't like. But there is a deep, abiding wisdom that I don't want to turn away from."

Ree gets up and tells her story of her fling with the FBI agent, and the whole room collapses in delight.

ONE EVENING MY OLD FRIEND Cyprian, who has been leading retreats and giving concerts in Beirut, in Jakarta, in southern India, brings onto the stage his whole band of "crazy friends": a Latina singer with an Indian name, the handsome high school teacher who plays guitar, other dharma brothers and sisters from the cabin where he's been living in Santa Cruz, doing hatha yoga and sitting zazen. They sing songs drawn from the Bhagavad Gita mixed with liturgy, Islamic chants set to tabla and sitar; in words or thoughts, the mixing of traditions can sound promiscuous, but in music it makes for a soaring harmony. There's no way I can stop getting to my feet and starting clapping, dancing, the infectious rhythms and melodies pulsing through me for day after long day.

One lunch, an entire meal is taken in silence, and the sense of intimacy, of intensity, builds till it seems ready to break.

SUCH A SENSE of repletion as I drive away: not the repletion I've come to know in my cell, but something more penetrating and surprising. So little seems to separate me from that Cuban woman with a Tibetan Buddhist practice, that executive from Southeast Asia. It's as if we've turned ourselves inside out, as in the silence, but collectively: our public selves are left on the highway, and we're sharing our innermost beings with unmet friends.

"IT'S SO WONDERFUL what you do here," a visitor tells a monk.

"We don't do anything!" he protests. "We make nothing happen."

"That's exactly it! Facilitating the nothing, but in a positive way. Creating the nothingness in which we become nothing. Giving us emptiness so we can be filled up."

I smile to hear my words issue from another's mouth.

Checking in to the monastery on the way back, I learn that a monk is gone. He lost his kidney in a hospital, but he was insistent about coming home for his final hours. Every day he shuffled into the chapel, on his cane, until one night he tried to rise from his bed. "I have somewhere to go."

"Stay here," said the monk who was tending to him. "Be calm."

"Thank you," he said, and by the morning he was dead.

At the gathering, I'd stumbled upon an email in my spam folder while checking my messages. I hadn't recognized the name on it, so I'd braced myself for a cyber scam or sales pitch.

Instead I'd found something invigorating: a message from Thérèse, the old woman who stays alone in a cabin in the valley next to the Hermitage. We've never spoken much, but her words from our last meeting, about the clarity she's found in solitude, go through me still; I wonder if she might in fact be the secret sage in the community, free to engage in undistracted contemplation while the monks bustle about their many duties.

She came across an old book of mine, she writes now, with unguarded warmth, and its title features both ladies and monks: might I have time to look in on her sometime when I'm on retreat?

One hot afternoon, I scramble down an unpaved slope at the far end of the enclosure, crowded with spare tires and the relics of dead cars, to find her waiting at her table above a plate of ginger cookies she's prepared in honor of our meeting. She's elegant as always, in black velvet jacket, a red Alice band around her soft white hair; her features remain delicate and very French. She hands me a cool moist towel to dry myself off. She's gathered two CDs to share, two diaries she keeps. She sets out a chilled bottle of water and glass for each of us.

The monks take pains to honor their promise to protect her till her final journey: one comes down every summer to secure her screen door from flies; another is deputed each week to wheel her up the steep slope to Eucharist. At Christmas she places lanterns around the trees, already lavish with her art and statues; the day of Jesus's birth

Learning from Silence

becomes a festival of lights, a celebration of spirits freed of all theology.

Now, as we talk, she glimpses the prior through the window, hastening down the hillside, white robes flying all around him. "We have a project!" she calls out, somewhat brusquely, as he draws closer. Startled, he turns around and goes back the way he came. Later, a withered-looking worker from up above, unsteady on his feet and flashing a grin that discloses few teeth, arrives to work on unplugging her toilet.

"When I got your message," Thérèse tells me now, eyes shining—she looks down at the yellow legal pad on which she's written all she doesn't want to forget—"it was as if I was being pierced. Pierced! I'm not an emotional person, but when I read your book I felt, 'God knows me. He understands me.' And when I received your email, it was like a sword of light coming through me. That's never happened before."

Her eyes are moist when she looks up.

"I'm sorry. You're a busy man, I know. I don't want to take away from your time in silence. But I felt I had to say this, and I couldn't say it in an email. This morning I had my English, but now . . ."

"I'm so pleased you thought to contact me."

"You can have a lifelong love affair," she says, "without ever touching. A *liaison* of the heart."

"Sometimes I think that's what this place is about."

She tells me of the monks she's always cherished because their hearts are wide open; others she calls "dry as dust." She shows me pictures she's taken over the years of her closest friends in the community, poems she's written, as if her place here is to preserve a spirit that might otherwise be forgotten.

When I get up to leave, her eyes are flashing. "I hope I will see you again." There's mischief in her voice. "My health is well-balanced, but I've had falls. I don't know when I'll be in my next home!"

AS I RESUME MY LIFE in the world, doors start swinging open on a whole community of hidden treasures. I have to fly to Singapore for my job, and I seek out the Islamic scholar of government from Oxford who pledged his allegiance to the Hermitage in his local mosque. Mark, not far away, the management consultant who regularly flies over to help the monks with their financial planning, invites me to lunch at his club, together with his delightfully bubbly Chinese wife. He's seen such suffering among the leading families of Asia that now he's completing a doctorate in counseling to see how he might help.

At the end of our lunch, he says, "I thought you might be interested in this," and hands me a book about Thomas

Merton's lifelong love affair from afar with the Camaldolese. It had been Merton who urged Rome to set up a Camaldolese house in California; he regularly asked permission to join the congregation, but as the superiors who kept denying him surely sensed, for a patron saint of restlessness, even a place of silent contemplation might lead only to new questions and a different set of hopes.

I start hearing from Deborah, a Presbyterian-raised spiritual director who showers me now with generous, eloquent letters about the books she loves, her trips to England, the monks she's especially close to. Have I read the new George Saunders? Underneath his zany surfaces, he's writing only about compassion; tending to the suffering. I pick up his latest stories and see them in a new light: she's right, as I've never had the patience to understand before. His work is about nothing other than suspending judgment and extending kindness towards the mocked and the downtrodden.

I had hoped, spending time in the Hermitage, to learn from the monks; but by now I'm gaining so much also from the fellow travelers met along the road. Like nobody else in my life they feel like instant comrades, worthy of deepest trust, if only because what we share sits at the very heart of us.

When Cyprian is asked how friends can help his monastery as winter storms cut it off again, he says, "You could offer material support to others in California—those who have lost their homes or their livelihoods, the indigent, the most vulnerable in the community." His family, in other words, is the world.

IN NARA ONE DAY, Hiroko and I are going over some of the friends we have, thinking of their graces and endearing quirks. The fog is thick this morning, which means that talk is very close; we're enfolded inside our tiny room.

So many people we know—maybe the same is true of me—want to seem worldly, and yet in that very act, betray their innocence. It's so often our unfallen-ness we disguise as diligently as our sins.

Then on to one of a couple's happiest tasks: to summon the qualities in one another we admire, which sometimes it takes an outsider's eye to see.

Hiroko offers some generous comments, and I say, "What do you think is the devil in me?"

"Your need to be alone."

"No, no. Not the angel. The bad part, the demon."

"Your need to be alone."

2.

I REALIZE, on my next trip up, that I'm in the unexpected position now of having an old friend serve as prior of the community. Burning-eyed Cyprian is one of the most talented souls I know, and for the last ten years he's earned a special dispensation to stay in a cabin ninety minutes to the north, taking his wisdom and his music around the world. Now, however, his brothers have found themselves obliged to elect a new prior—"We often say, 'Jesus couldn't do this job!'" one of them confesses—and the only candidate they can find is Father Robert, already seventy-five. He tries his best, but soon realizes that his health is not up to months-long discussions on how to repair the roofs and where to find eighty thousand dollars a year for diesel fuel. All eyes turn to the uncommonly vigorous and electric brother up the coast.

One evening I steal into the enclosure to join my friend for dinner. There's a candle on the altar in his simple cell, and next to it a Buddha. Bamboo lanterns and, on the wall, a scroll depicting Jesus in the lotus position. As if to remind him of the life he's given up, a poster of *On the Road*.

"So, what are you working on now?" he asks as he expertly tosses a glistening, fresh salad.

I'm almost embarrassed to answer. "Well, actually"—how to say this to a monk, as someone outside his faith?—"I'm writing an essay on the Song of Songs. A friend is putting together a book on the Bible, and I thought it might be good to have one piece written by someone who's not a believer. I've always . . ."

"Right on!" cries Cyprian, darting across the room to fetch a CD. "Look at what I was listening to just before you came!" It's Palestrina, putting the Bible's book of arising to soaring song. "If I had to listen to only one piece of music in the world," he says, returning to sit on the floor around our small table, "it would be this." He has his Bible open at the lyrics.

The Church had wanted to ban harmonies in the sixteenth century, he explains, because they can blur words that are designed to be holy. But Palestrina found a way to layer sounds so that many voices could be heard at once, yet not a syllable lost.

"It's the most written-about book in the Bible," he exclaims, on fire. "By the ancient Church Fathers. For the rabbis, it was not just the Song of Songs, but the Holy of Holies. Some see it as speaking for the marriage of God and Jerusalem, or of Christ and the Church. But for the mystics, it simply told the love story of the soul and whatever is divine.

"Bernard of Clairvaux," he says, barely pausing for breath, "wrote forty-three sermons about the Song of Songs."

I notice all the works of scholarship on his shelves: on self-giving and Hinduism, on mysticism and Buddhism and Islam. In Italian and with references in Latin and Greek. At his installation as prior, a few months earlier, he'd said, "Our job is to stay in the cauldron without getting burned."

I try to explain how the Song of Songs and the Book of Job keep going round in my head; sometimes I feel that everything I need to know is in them. Rapture and humility; the joy of exulting in all the sensory beauty of the world, and the importance of recalling that none of it will play out as we expect.

The meadows all around, alight with golden poppies, and the flames that could at any moment overwhelm what looks to be a simple group of devoted souls trying to give themselves up to what's beyond them.

IN THE MORNINGS NOW, I always awaken to Handel: his soaring anthems seem with ever-renewing freshness to be announcing the coming not just of light, but of a transformative new world. "For unto us a child is born" and "Ev'ry valley shall be exalted" carry me up into the heavens, and to a perspective from which even the gray fields of England seem to gleam in summer light. An earthly Song of Songs, I decide.

At night, sitting alone in our small apartment in the dark, waiting for Hiroko to come back from work, I turn more often to Leonard Cohen. His dense, unsparing songs refuse to believe that the world is soluble or any transport permanent; they push, unflinchingly, into bafflement and betrayal, even sin, the order of punishment he never shies away from. Here, I think, is Buddhist practice: simply, systematically picking apart every inconstancy to remind us that we cannot count on anything other than a mind that is prepared to live calmly with all that it cannot control.

No wonder, I think, one rich November morning, I choose to spend my autumns in Japan, a seasoned culture built around impermanence that has, for fourteen hundred years or more, refined a sense of how to live with suffering and loss and the many illusions the mind can throw up. And every spring, by instinct, find my way back to New Camaldoli, which I associate with resurrection, hope, the light that floods the chapel.

Both, I notice, are offering a hallelujah. The Los Angeles choir that offers renditions of Handel's *Messiah* at

Christmas for the inhabitants of Skid Row sometimes concludes, I hear, with a solo performance of Leonard's "cold and broken" hallelujah.

WHEN I MAKE the long drive now, under darkening skies, through thickening traffic, down to see my Zen friend in his duplex, he, too, is beginning to look shaky. He's been diagnosed with something for which there is no cure. Of course, he offers with unsleeping irony, we're all suffering from something for which there is no cure. But this is specific, and depleting. He heats up bagels for me from Montreal—the only ones worth eating, he assures me—and opens up his refrigerator to show me the medical marijuana in pretzel and popcorn form he's been given to deal with the pain.

In his little bare study—only a few photos along the wall, of his mother and father, an old friend, two dogs—we sit in front of his huge desktop, and he plays me the album he'll be releasing soon, with a title only Leonard Cohen could love: *Popular Problems*. Then we head to a tiny Mediterranean café that he favors nearby; a stranger accosts him with astonished delight in a back alleyway, and he bows before the young man as if before his teacher.

His old Japanese friend is in the hospital now, and it doesn't look good; after I get home, Leonard writes to say that the tiny 107-year-old man, who had outlived many an earlier death sentence, took his last breath hours after the two of us finished lunch. Two days later, he goes on, his only sibling, Esther, was rushed to the hospital in New York and he had to fly over to be with her. Six weeks later, she, too, is gone.

I remember what he'd said with clenched passion in the intimacy of his bare room. "That's what this practice, this whole life is about. Cleaning the bottom of a 107-year-old man. Helping him go to the bathroom when he can't do it himself. Taking care of the diapers."

There were three in the hospital tending to their friend in his final days, one of the other two tells me. But it was elegant and impeccable Leonard who insisted on getting up to take care of the mess when the abbot inadvertently soiled himself.

MORE AND MORE NOW, when I return to Big Sur, I begin slipping into the enclosure, as if I half belong there; sometimes to walk all the way to the muddy end, to head down the hidden slope to where Thérèse lives in her fairy-tale cottage, among her secret shrines and the lights she's scattered around the forest; sometimes stopping off in the little "rec room" behind the chapel where the monks watch Monty Python on Sunday nights or get together with visiting friends. Cyprian invites me there for overpoweringly strong tea—Assam mixed with Darjeeling—and we chat under the poster of his favorite film, *Of Gods and Men*, the movie commemorating a small community of Catholic monks in Algeria who gave up their lives to try to protect their Islamic neighbors from terrorists.

I've been listening to U2's anthems of uplift and I ask him about his life as a young musician, touring with covers of famous numbers. U2 had to be close to his heart, using its huge global platform to disseminate songs about devotion and taking on the Devil; its members seem almost to exult in sharing the "uncool" ideas of service and prayer. Bono sometimes hangs a cross around the mic as the band exits the stage, to the sound of Psalm 40; I've heard that members of the band fly to New Mexico to receive spiritual direction from Richard Rohr, the Franciscan priest who writes some of his radical, mystical books in the same trailer where I've so often stayed.

"I was just listening to Eddie Vedder, in concert," I tell the prior, who surely craves occasional reports from the world he knew, "and he ended with Bob Marley. 'Redemption Song.'"

My friend pulls down his guitar from the back of the room, and before I know it, I'm hearing, "Emancipate yourselves from mental slavery . . ." and the reminder that only we can free ourselves.

. . .

SOMETIMES I WORRY for my friends: all across the world, every kind of monastery and convent is being shuttered. Lifelong commitments are too difficult in the age of short attention spans; many—I'm too perfect an example—love to partake of a few days of absolute clarity and calm but shy away from giving ourselves up to the all-consuming hard work of a lifetime of surrender and obedience. The Hermitage began taking oblates, or lay members of the community who vow to honor the principles associated with the monks, in 1989, and the seven who were here when first I arrived now number almost eight hundred, from every religion and corner of the globe; the number of actual monks, however, is dwindling, and for young novices it can be hard to stay in what is, ever more, a community of very old men.

So what can I do? I try to offer what I can, and often I meet friends who I think might benefit from the unbroken silence that pulses here, beyond the reach of opinions or theories. But variations on it can be found in every monastery and convent, and sometimes I'll just urge people to find the place that's nearest to them, since it's the stillness that liberates more than the location.

When first I began coming here, the prior's challenge was an excess of new blood: more and more eager young men who had to be fed and housed, so many that Father

Robert, almost overwhelmed, wondered if he should send them off to other houses in need of reinforcements, and the order opened, for a few years, a monastery in New Hampshire. Now, for no apparent reason, I see many of even the most devout postulants return to secular lives, and I wonder how the rest of us will fare in the absence of these "candle-bearers," as Merton called them, who give up their peace so we can enjoy ours.

ONE DAZZLING AFTERNOON IN SPRING, I arrive at the bookstore, exhilarated. In a world of commotion I need more than ever to be reminded of what endures. As I walk towards the cash register to check in, I notice there's a small woman there, speaking in whispers to the monk on duty. When at last she steps away, I see a frail-looking soul, almost ashen, who seems very close to disappearing.

"I'm in room 7, I think," I tell the monk and wait for him to complete the paperwork. Then I turn round and catch sight of the woman, with her short gray hair, thin spectacles, a shockingly pallid countenance.

"Ree?" I say.

She nods.

"I can't believe it!" I wrap her in my arms. "I haven't been here for months! I'm here only for three minutes to check in. And I walk right into you! It's a miracle."

She smiles wanly. She still likes to come for Easter, she says in a voice I can barely catch, but it's hard to raise the funds for a long stay. She's found a motel two hours to the north where a kindly Filipina offers her a monthly rate. She drives down when she can.

"I can't believe I get to see you again! My long-lost friend."

She gives a weak smile and shuffles out.

ONE MONTH LATER, I check in to a little hotel in the mountains and get word that Ree is very sick; it won't be long now. The Crohn's disease that has been plaguing her for years, sometimes reducing her to unimaginable pain, refuses to subside.

I sit down on my bed and record a greeting to send her. But what good are words when all someone in distress really needs is a warm hand, or a shoulder to rest on?

I don't even know if they reach her in time; she's gone by daybreak.

IT'S SO UNFATHOMABLE, Cyprian agrees; he's become an expert at tending to the dying. For so long, I'd admired monastics for daring to contemplate their own extinction. But now I'm coming to see how they have to face up to what can be an even harder lot: the gradual falling away of the friends they've been serving for decades. Cyprian, as prior, has to visit every one of them in hospital, as a parent might; he has to console them when they tremble and lead the wake that follows.

When more than five million cubic yards of rock and dirt collapse into the ocean just to the south of the Hermitage, and, not much later, a bridge to the north gives out, a monk has a fall and needs to be helicoptered out to a hospital two and a half hours away by car. The secret back road, the Road of Birth, is open only after dark. Every night Cyprian makes the five-hour drive beside the sheer drop, one moment of inattention likely fatal. When the phone lines give out, he can communicate with the outside world only by walkie-talkie.

"There has been a real spirit of joy and co-operation pervading New Camaldoli," he writes, in the rare message he's able to send out through a colleague. The monks miss all their friends, and revenue is down to zero. But in the uninterrupted quiet they find a spirit of worship, and of fellowship, that brings them even closer to what they love.

WHEN FINALLY I get back to the place, thanks to that secret entrance, I seek my friend out. I'm not sure I've ever met anyone who can do so much at once: he's still writing erudite books, recording new music, giving homilies several times a week and leading retreats when he can. He maintains his yoga practice, and I never forget seeing his lean and elegant form early one Sunday morning taking his seven-mile run along the empty highway at the bottom of the hill.

He, too, has suffered a small collapse, and his doctors tell him to go easy on himself. He knows he has to do that to be useful to his "family," and I for one keep thinking of the life of constant stimulation and growth he gave up in order to look after his brothers and ensure that their home survives.

"You know that song, 'If It Be Your Will,'" I say, thinking of the other monk-singer I visit who humbles me with all he's given up.

Cyprian nods; there's little he doesn't know.

"I think of that young adventurer who was so eager to chart his own destiny," I say, "in all the early songs. That sense of surrender that's the real act of love . . ." and then I realize that I don't need to say another word. The man in front of me knows sacrifice from the inside out.

"I THINK I WAS always destined to end up where I am," says my new friend Fu, the tall, steady, piercing-eyed abbess of a Zen center across the hills. "Even though I don't believe in destiny."

"Thomas Merton said that it's less important to find

God than to open yourself up enough so you can be found by him."

She opens her eyes wide. "I like that! I remember when I was young, I loved ecstatic poetry. I felt it, in the center of my being. But you can't live in ecstatic poetry. You can't live on Everest. It's got no snack bars, as I tell the kids. You have to come back and do the dishes."

I remember the time she told me that when she began Zen practice, almost fifty years before, she was suddenly asked to cook for a hundred and fifty people. No preparation, no warning. She'd had to learn, as all the students did, how to clean, how to cook, how to raise funds, how to help with accounts. Now she's responsible for dozens of young students in a center just north of San Francisco, many of them lost and in great need.

"It's very interesting to me," she said, "this dual citizenship. Between the stars and the stones."

THROUGH MY NEW FRIEND I'd seen a very different side to Zen practice than the unrelenting Marine Corps regimen I'd witnessed when I visited Leonard on his mountaintop. Fu never spoke of enlightenment; only of service. Her practice wasn't about getting the better of self; it was simply about dissolving all distinctions between me and you. Love, in effect, and caring. Every time she sent me an email—"I try to add something every time, even in the title, just to make it personal and fun"—she signed off, "Your Fu."

"All these questions," she says to me, marveling, one day. "'Where am I going? What is my home? Who am I?' Well, that last one doesn't seem to be so interesting!"

She gives a rich laugh; she never leaves the earth entirely.

She was once in a sacred place in Navajoland, she tells me, and spent all night under the stars, the rare visitor permitted to sleep there. "And all night I was hungry with these big questions. Thinking about the universe, all of it. And out of nowhere—this has happened to me only twice in my life—I heard a strong male voice saying, 'You will never know!'

"And I just felt this amazing relief."

"That voice was in you."

She shrugs. "My father worked in radio here and there, and he had a beautiful, resonant voice."

I tell her about my own uncanny moments, when the roof opens up and I'm reminded of all I can never know.

"They're just these little drops," she says, "these little sparkles. And if you join them all together, like beads in a necklace, maybe that's our life."

"But don't you think we need the shadows, too?" I say. "The memory of mistakes and wounds that stay with us forever?"

I pause. "Maybe the sparkles are there to balance out the traumas?"

She looks at me directly, this slim, clear woman with erect posture and cropped white hair and black robes, in no hurry to reduce life to explanations. "I don't even know how much I have forgotten."

"And all of it disappears in any case. There for a moment, and only in the mind."

"You can't dwell on things," Fu agrees. "That's the heart of Zen practice. Not dwelling."

She cites a line from the thirteenth-century teacher Dogen: all he knows is the sound of black rain on the tiles of the roof.

"And even that doesn't last," I say.

3.

THE PRIOR LIGHTS UP the minute I introduce him to Hiroko. Women are not permitted inside the monks' enclosure after dark, but he makes sure to come down that evening to the terrace of my trailer—Hiroko has laid claim to the next cottage down, so we almost feel we're staying together—and over very strong tea, all three of us talk until the path up the slope is silver in the moonlight and we're encircled by stars.

Next day, as we're browsing through the bookstore—blue earrings and silver crosses; necklaces and vials of perfume as well as books from every continent—one of the men who helps manage finances for the monks comes in.

"Congratulations!" he cries as soon as he sees us.

"Thanks." I don't know what he's referring to.

"On your wedding!"

"Oh, thank you." We've actually been together almost thirty years by now, but Hiroko's job hasn't allowed her to come and stay in the Hermitage before.

"You two look like you're on your honeymoon."

"Don't they say that places like this are a constant renewal?"

I'VE OFTEN BROUGHT Hiroko up to the Hermitage when we're driving along Highway 1, to walk along the monastery road, to enjoy the view, more or less unmatched along the coast, the natural cathedral that is Big Sur given point and focus by the bells. She's walked around the chapel in wonder and come to see that instead of regarding it as a rival, she can make it a part of her life, too.

Now, as we enter the church, she watches, with fascination, the monks as they bow before the altar, then wave incense above us all, scatter water over our bowed heads. "I'm Japanese," I heard her tell an American friend recently. "We believe the name is not so important. If I'm in Japan, I pray inside a temple. In California I go into a church. Not so different."

Never one to lose the chance for human contact, she follows the others into the rotunda as communion begins and I have no choice but to go along with her. She takes the wafer from a priest's hand, she drinks the wine. She enthusiastically wishes peace to everyone around us and shares hugs and handshakes at the end of the ceremony.

We return to our seats in the chapel and a big, bearded monk comes over to meet her, glowing. "Welcome! We weren't even sure you existed!"

She beams, extends a hand. "I'm so happy to meet you."

Another comes over. "We heard about you from Pico, but we never got the chance to see you before."

Another, and then another.

When at last we file out into the daylight, the hexagonal window in front of us offering an expansive view of the coast stretching out to north and south, Hiroko looks at me, overwhelmed.

"For thirty years I thought you were an only child. Now I see you have all these brothers!"

A FEW SEASONS LATER, we contrive to spend an entire month around Big Sur, in one sought-after sanctuary after another.

"What do you think?" I ask as we head home at last.

She starts talking about the famous retreat-place with the radiant lawns, the golden bodies, a candlelit Buddha above the crashing surf. "It's like humans' ideas of Heaven."

"Which is not so good?"

"Which means it's a little like Hell."

"What about the other one?"

"So beautiful. But so many kids." Such places draw the wounded and confused, those driven by an ache; sometimes retreat-houses can feel like hospitals for broken hearts.

"And the Hermitage?"

"True Heaven." By which, I think she means, no words; and the people around us do not as a rule seem to be looking for enlightenment or transport or mystic truth. They've simply found a place to renew themselves in quiet.

THE DAY I TURN FIFTY-EIGHT I wake up with the sun, devour my usual breakfast—"Horse biscuits," as Hiroko pronounces delightedly of my three ill-tasting cereal bars—and drive across town. I've been asked to wait at a deli and a car will collect me and bring me to the big estate down the road.

We pass through its gates, and I'm taken to an expansive greenroom filled with shelf after shelf of books. A producer prepares me for the interview to come and, with what I've come to see as characteristic kindness, warns me that there'll be some rapid-fire questions at the end. She shares the questions in advance, so I won't be taken by surprise.

When I sit out in the garden for the interview, however, the questions at the end of the hour-long talk turn out to be completely different from the ones I'd been prepared for; perhaps they were meant for the guest who came after me.

"Do you have a definition of God?" the host suddenly inquires.

"Reality," I say, not thinking.

She looks at me, taken aback. "Wow!" She shakes her head. "I have been asking that question for four years and that is the first time I've had that answer. 'God is reality.'" She tries it out on her tongue again, as if in another, near-silent "Wow."

Later, I think that if I had been prepared, or if I'd thought about it for a hundred hours, I could never have come up with something closer to what I believe. Did I mean that reality is the deity before which we have to kneel and bow, as a Buddhist might say? Did I mean that divinity is real, not something out of fancy, as my Christian friends would hold?

It hardly matters. I had no time to perfect an answer, so what came out of me was true.

THROUGH ALL THE STORMS and changes in the world, my friend Thérèse remains agile and playful. She bakes ginger cookies for me every time I come to visit, and sends bags of them home for my mother. She keeps her legal pad handy whenever we talk so not a single thought—from me or from her—will escape; she screens a movie she loves for me and Hiroko in her bedroom—"I have now seen it twenty-three times!"—and gives us stirring accounts of the monks who light her up.

Many of them are growing very old now: one is so alive with all that he longs to share that he's taken to the road to lead retreats on the monastic within us all; another has returned to his first cloistered home, across the country.

Through all of this, Thérèse keeps shining, like a candle in the fog. When once I come to visit her, sporting my usual tatty jeans with the knees worn away and broken sneakers under the mustard-yellow shirt I'm still wearing after twenty-five years of retreats, she looks alarmed.

"Where is your holey sweater?"

"I'm not allowed to wear it while Hiroko is nearby."

"But you wear it still, I hope?"

"Don't worry. Holey-ness never goes away."

OFTEN, WHEN I EMAIL my friend the prior now, I hear of the latest challenge. One day, not seeing one of the brothers at Vigils, Cyprian had knocked on the man's gate.

When there'd been no answer, he'd gone in to find his friend in bed, unable to move and communicating only with hand signals. As the fading man neared the end, two days later, it was up to the prior and the monk's sister to make the hard decisions.

Nothing can really prepare him for such trials, my friend admits. Even gut feeling isn't always an answer, his spiritual director has advised him. What should he say to that ardent young soul so eager to boost the numbers in the enclosure who probably would be disappointed by the life? What to do with the older monk—his senior—who, told by a doctor that time is short, announces loudly that he doesn't want to die? What of that homeless person who's climbed all the way up the hill to the bookstore— two steep miles—because surely a man of God would never turn a man in need away?

A big part of his job, the young head of a Zen community writes to me, involves playing the part, putting on the brave face that everybody else requires. He is, in effect, a general giving courage to his troops, performing a strength he doesn't always feel.

But to be a wise leader, you have to be human. And wisdom cannot come at the expense of feeling. When he walked down for a shy monk's funeral, Cyprian tells me, it was to find one young monk sobbing on a bench. That wasn't the only sobbing heard that night.

Learning from Silence

. . .

ONE EVENING, in the silent hours, the phone in our apartment in Japan starts ringing and I learn that my mother has had a stroke. I hurry across the ocean to be by her side, and do what I can to ensure that she can stay in the house she loves, looked after day and night. But as the years go on, inevitably, both mind and body begin to come apart. When I join her at her dinner table, she looks right through me, as if I'm the one who's become a ghost. In her pain, she starts calling out, this most stoical and self-possessed of souls, for her mother.

"She cries in the night," reports Susana, who sleeps at the foot of her old friend's bed. "She's scared; she can see the other side."

I'm determined to make sure that she not be moved to a facility—she would wilt quickly if she did—and thus I face a twenty-first-century predicament: the more I want to protect my mother, the more I have to travel away from her to earn money to pay for her health-care needs.

Wherever I am, though, emails keep arriving from my spirited and wise new friend in her cottage; always they guide me into a clearing where the sun is bright.

She writes to me of how "my thirty years at the Hermitage have been pure joy, in sculpting first and then carving the wilderness into seven sanctuaries." She tells of planning a birthday party for a monk and how "the sycamores are disrobing in my canyon . . . each leaf has a personal way to waltz all the way to the ground."

She reports, a little later, on the party she held, "with a shower of soap bubbles in all sizes, reflecting the sunset." Outside, she'd placed fifty lanterns and soon they "were showing their soul in the dark." When she signs off, it's as "The old lantern, Thérèse."

In the very last letter she sends to me, recalling the unsightly clothes I've been wearing over decades in the Hermitage, she concludes, "Yes. We have to see the holey green sweater as a proof of permanence."

ONE LATE AUTUMN DAY, I'm back in Japan, for my job, when suddenly emails begin flooding in. "We got an emergency alert," writes a nun friend, "and the wind is howling. I'm worried about your mom." Sam, visiting from Big Sur, sends a message to say he's ready to drive up then and there to rescue my mother. "I can see the flames from down here," writes Kim, in alarm. I conjure up, in my mind's eye, walls of orange above the ridge half a mile from the house, feel the air tighten around me. For someone with asthma— my mother, say—it will soon become impossible to breathe.

They're calling it the Cave Fire, Hollye tells me, as if to invoke the Painted Cave Fire, in exactly the same area, the blaze that reduced our home to rubble.

Learning from Silence

So many of us are living where humans were never meant to live, disrupting an ageless and essential life cycle; fires invite the sunlight in by thinning out the lower branches of trees, they clear the way for new seeds and roots. When I mentioned to Father Robert how mountain lions were seen now on our road and even walking through the center of town, he'd reminded me gently that it's not they who are intruding on our territory, but we on theirs.

For now, what can I do? I walk out of our room and into the local park. Across the neighborhood and down the hidden flight of stairs that leads to an older world of rice paddies and wooden houses. Then up to the nearest shrine.

I throw coins in a wooden box. I pull a rope to summon the Shinto gods. Then, putting my hands together, I close my eyes. I see the fountain in the courtyard in Big Sur, in the sunlight. The thangka in the chapter room that beats like a healthy heart. The tiny candle in the glass bowl that seems never to give out.

I DON'T SLEEP well that night, and when I awaken, I do what I never do: go online to check my messages. "It's a beautiful day here in Santa Barbara," kind and peaceful Carl writes; the winds have subsided and the fire seems to be receding.

I calm down and go about my day. Three hours later, another message, this time from a helpful friend: I need to call our insurance company. A claims representative has reported a structure burned to the ground on our property.

I try to call my mother, who has safely been evacuated, but she is confused, and hardly knows there's been a fire. Other friends assure me that the house seems still to be standing. Then selfless Carl drives up and reports that our entire water pump, not many yards from the front door, is black skeleton and ash. As soon as the fire began to be contained, our electric company, which had turned off power in the area to prevent an accident, turned it on again and the sudden surge set our pump ablaze.

The rest I learn only months later. Two neighbors, forming a volunteer fire patrol, had been driving up and down the road as the crisis promised to subside, to make sure everyone was okay. They'd seen the flames around our house and, though lacking professional equipment, had stayed by our water pump for three long hours, deploying hoses to keep the fire at bay.

Finally, professional firefighters came by, and the brave volunteers were free to go home as a helicopter arrived to douse the flames. Our house, perhaps my mother's life, saved by two openhearted strangers.

"WE ARE THE FIRE CREATURE," I hear the fire historian Stephen Pyne declare in a documentary, referring to the Bible and its talk of "trying fires," the flames that test us.

Often, he points out, the only thing that survives a conflagration is a chimney.

Fire is nature's agent of rebirth. It replenishes wild places much as I replenish myself by sitting in silence. Out go built-up leaves, in comes open space for animals. Meadows and pine trees and manzanita cannot survive in its absence.

It's all the trees that humans plant that disrupt the natural cycle, many now tell us, giving wildfires today their unnatural ferocity. Before long the papers are reporting eighty-five deaths in a town called Paradise, with people stuck in their cars on a single narrow road, flames on every side of them. One in every three in California alone—ten million—live in what is now called the "wildfire zone," knowing that much of the landscape we love cannot live unless flames sweep through, remaking everything.

IN THE SUMMER OF 2018, the Hermitage celebrates its sixtieth year of existence; through a magical convergence, its birthday comes one month after the prior, Cyprian, turns sixty, born as he auspiciously was on the feast day of St. Romuald. A festive picnic in the courtyard draws dozens of old friends, and then there's a concert in the chapel; I'm thrilled to see that kindly Father Robert, who first welcomed me to the place twenty-seven years before and who used to let Elizabeth the cat into his bed every morning for three minutes of "quality time," can celebrate the home where he's been living for almost all its sixty years. He had a fall, but now he's shuffling back into chapel, attended by a fellow monk, and remembering, perhaps, the cowshed and barn that were what he had to live with when first he arrived.

"We don't want to be traditional or modern or anything," I recall Cyprian saying, and I'd realized that it was precisely the place's freedom from the passing moment that moved me so; the monks seem content to wear the same habit and observe many of the same practices of fifty generations of fathers and brothers. They show no eagerness to adapt to every passing fad or to assume that deepest truths ever grow outdated.

The following month, Cyprian gets to enjoy a sabbatical, and I'm glad to think he can catch the rest his body so clearly needs; he'll even get to help lead a workshop at the Zen monastery fourteen miles away.

I write to him to report on my own workshop there, and to rejoice in his brief taste of freedom, and he writes back that there'll be no workshop and no release: Father Robert has been diagnosed with a brain hemorrhage, and he's back in hospital. Cyprian has to be with his old friend and teacher, the one who brought him here and guided him towards the priorship.

"I'm the only family some of these guys have now," he

tells me. I think of the dying monk who said to a friend of mine, "Father Prior is a very good mother."

I don't know what to write back, so I simply tell my friend how lucky I feel to have some choice at every moment; while many of my friends are happy tuning in to the news, I'm so glad I get to watch the radiance outside my window. To take a walk among the quail and squirrels. Perhaps it's even the Hermitage that taught me how to direct my gaze.

The prior writes back, overflowing as ever with spirit and new ideas. "Like love, sometimes hope is a choice," he writes. "Of course you will know the great Cornel West quote about that, yes? The difference between hope and optimism?" The former is a leap beyond all evidence while the other is simply an attempt to work with what it knows.

"It's a choice I make," he continues. "There's a beautiful album I heard the other day on Spotify, mostly flute, a little vocal. Called 'I Will Not Be Sad in This World.'"

4.

In my own life, I find myself more and more, in the shower every morning, panning across scenes from the Hermitage in my head. Seeing the little cabin on the dirt road, the candle flickering in its glass bowl. Mary and her Child, compassion and trust, above the light in the long blue glass and the blue-green plate on the floor in which visitors place handwritten prayers.

A new friend, from Coca-Cola, whom I met at a marketing summit, sends me two snapshots of the place and I prop them up on my tiny desk. Streams of light coming down in the rotunda; blue sky above blue water through the hexagonal window outside.

In recent years, the monks have gained a new big boss, and a part of me rejoices that, in place of the theologian who was Pontiff, there's a man from the south who has worked as a janitor, a nightclub bouncer and a chemical technician. "We need someone like the Dalai Lama in our own church," Father Robert had said once over lunch as I spoke of all I'd learned from the Tibetan.

He must have rejoiced when he read the personal creed of the Pope, who held that his faith should be not an NGO, but a love story. "I believe in the goodness of others," Francis had written, as he prepared for his ordination. "I believe I wish to love a lot . . . I believe in the burning death of each day, from which I flee, but which smiles at me, inviting me to accept her." The new Pope prayed, I read, not for an answer to any problem, but only for the courage to live with the unanswerable.

ONE BRIGHT WINTER DAY, we learn of a virus forcing quarantine in China. People are dying, we hear, and, days later, the entire globe enters an enforced retreat of sorts as a coronavirus spreads with every whisper. Lockdown is announced in California, and, twenty hours later, my mother is rushed to the hospital in an ambulance; she's losing blood, at a frightening rate. As soon as she's released, I take three flights through eerily deserted airports to care for her for the next six months.

Hiroko follows me over, and one day we find ourselves free at last to drive out of town for a day; we head straight to the Hermitage. But the private road up from the highway is completely blocked off. Somebody has draped a cloth over the sign that mentions a bookstore and retreat-house. I steer around the roadblock and drive up towards the chapel. Everything is desolate and hushed. Not a single figure visible. Then we hear someone handling paperwork in a side office.

"Is it okay for us to be here?" I call out.

"No," comes a woman's voice, urgent. "You must go now, please."

TWO MONTHS LATER, in August, the place does open, but only partially. It's a curious time in the world's life: the chapel has to remain closed, and only one room in every two is open, to contain infection. The entire planet has been humbled, reminded of how much lies outside even the strongest being's control. We drive around the roadblock again and steer slowly up the winding road.

The silence at the top is more absolute than ever, enveloping. We glimpse not a soul as we drive up. Farther up the coast, down the coast, across the world, hospitals and morgues are filling up beyond capacity. Nobody is counting on tomorrow.

Here all is radiant peace. A sign outside the kitchen reminds us to keep "one cow apart" while lining up for lunch. When I meet with Hiroko our first morning there for a walk, however—she's in one of the comfy cottages, I prefer the bare retreat-room—she's uncharacteristically restless.

"I was scared last night."

"This is the safest place I know."

"I know. But I felt something. Something dark."

"Don't worry. This is the home of calm." We meander towards the last bench and sit there, listening to the ceaseless music of the sea. The best cure for anxiety, Cyprian had written to us all, is taking care of others.

The afternoon passes without incident, but as we take our last walk of the day, the sun flooding the hills with red and gold, we hear a chopper flying over, very fast, to the north. I've come to dread the sound: in places like this, it generally means looking for someone lost in the wilderness or the proximity of fire.

Another helicopter comes whirring across the horizon, no less urgent; I recall how when I was stuck within the flames outside our family home, I could hear a chopper's blades up above, though the smoke was so thick that the first responders in the clouds could not see me, nor I them.

"No wonder you were scared," I say.

Hiroko nods. "I felt something evil."

WE RETURN TO OUR ROOMS. When I step out of my cell next morning, I smell smoke.

"There must be a fire," I tell Hiroko when we meet for lunch. But the monks know nothing of any disturbance—only a conflagration up in Carmel, fifty miles to the north—and I try not to get agitated as planes start speeding overhead and midsummer blue turns to haze.

After lunch, we drive, as planned, down to the highway and start to head home. Less than two hours later, a man on a property right next to the Hermitage sets off a huge fire. He's tending an illegal cannabis farm—I remember Ree's tale of all the NO TRESPASSING signs she'd seen when she first came up here—and panicked as the authorities closed in on him.

By nightfall, all Big Sur is ablaze. Nearly every one of the monks evacuates again; most of them hasten south to a satellite hermitage they've set up 105 miles down the coast. Poor Thérèse, now ninety-four, has to be hurried out with kind Vickie, the woman who is now looking after her full-time; she's already survived one helicopter evacuation, after sudden worries about her health.

For four weeks, as the fire blazes, three monks, together with four workers, stay behind to rescue their home, and ours. Firefighters as ever risk their lives to try to protect every human structure, especially the Hermitage, managing to keep the flames to one side of the highway.

From within the blaze, the prior keeps all friends of the monastery informed with regular bulletins, calmly noting "a lot of pulsing light and occasional flash." There is a "definite smell of smoke everywhere," he writes, and sometimes the flames can be seen at the top of the hill right above the cells. One hundred and twenty-eight thousand acres are being laid waste.

"Other than that," he continues, "all is quiet, and the bell calls us to morning prayers." The three monks are still maintaining all the Offices, he writes, in the chapter room, and they have much to be grateful for.

"Blessed day all," he signs off his update.

BY THE NEXT TIME we drive up, two months later, the entire landscape is a burn victim. The slopes are charred horribly—bare black branches on black hills—and the soil seems scarred and wounded. We can see where the devastation reached the very edge of the property, as if the elements were scribbling defiant graffiti across the surface we're so keen to keep clean. On one side of the highway everything is black, infernal; on the other, bright slopes run towards a calm blue sea.

Already, golden pampas grass is covering some slopes, as arbitrary as after any zigzagging flames; but one of the monks who stayed back tells us, "If I'd known what it would be like, I would never have volunteered. I had what they called a silent heart attack, the doctors later told me."

He did volunteer, though, ready to die for the place that affords so many of the rest of us peace. Now he shakes his head in sympathy for the "poor guy" who set the fire off.

WHEN NEXT HIROKO and I scramble our way down to Thérèse's never-never cottage—she is away now, needing medical care—her warm and constantly smiling protector, Vickie, says, "We were very comfortable in the hermitage down south. But I had two mandatory evacuation orders at the same time as I had mandatory stay-at-home orders."

"That sounds like real life," I say. In Japan, days unfold just as they always do—trains and elevators crowded, children at school and parents at work—even as the government deems the pandemic a state of emergency. Everyday life and emergency may not be far apart.

THE LONG SEASON of the coronavirus surprises us all because of the doors it opens as well as the many, many that it closes. There's no denying the terror and the grief: more than seven million people lose their lives across the planet and economies large and small are shattered. My regally composed mother continues her slow collapse—"Why aren't you my mother?" she cries, eyes wide in horror, as she sees Hiroko coming in to tend to her—and the selfless young women who look after her, night and day, bring the virus into our home, along with their own many losses. Every kind of certainty is dissolved.

Yet the displacing interlude of stillness makes many things possible. I start taking walks up the road behind my mother's house; unable to go to the health club, I now go all the way to the end of the road, twenty minutes away, as I have not done in more than fifty years here.

I see peacocks fanning their bright tails on a neighbor's driveway. I watch the golden light of early morning irradiate the hills, while valleys remain in deepest shadow. I turn to see the sun scintillant on the ocean in the distance, the sky so sharp and blue I can make out the ridges in the islands far beyond.

Hiroko grows close to birds. She names the hummingbird who comes fluttering around her as she sits on a terrace, practicing yoga at first light, "Hay-ter." We walk around the lagoon near the university—again, unknown to me after half a century here—and watch cormorants flying low above the water, pelicans sharing an outcropping with seagulls. A snow-white egret stalks the shallows, all but motionless.

On the beach nearby are sandpipers, and, one bright afternoon, dolphins barely thirty feet away. We find a cormorant, exhausted after a dinnertime hunt, simply standing on the beach, feathers rumpled, dazed, and from that moment on, Hiroko cannot resist the dark birds whose form Satan assumed as he looked down on Eve in Paradise. We place a feeder on the terrace next to the dining room table, and every time wind-whirring birds begin sipping from it, my mother, however tired or weak or confused, lights up and calls, "Look! A little hummingbird!"

The season of taking nothing for granted opens our eyes to the beauty we've been sleepwalking past for most of our days. It brings into sharp relief what we really care about. It makes many of us rethink our lives and realize that maybe we don't want—or need—to go back to the blind and dizzy rush we've known before. In a curious way, in the heart of a trembling world, we're living a little as we might in the silence of the monastery.

WHEN THE PANDEMIC LIFTS, I start going back, as often as before, to my trusted friend, as I think of it. I hardly recognize the boy who first came here, half a lifetime ago, so fresh and wide open; yet the sentences I write, on every visit, are exactly the same cries of affirmation and joy that he once penned. So many of my friends from around the Hermitage are gone, but something of the best of them remains. The views through the windows still put my passing hopes and ideas, my anxious thoughts in place.

To find something you can't doubt, I realize, may be the closest that some of us need to get to faith.

I remember, as I settle into my cell one cold day, the time when Cyprian invited me to dinner, "with some money we got for Christmas." I could barely see his battered station wagon as I walked out into the rain, after dark; another winter storm was remaking the landscape, till almost everything was erased in thick fog.

I'd begun to understand by then what the commitment to obedience really meant. Not simply obedience to God, or even the Superior, or all the imperfect and sometimes exasperating men you have to live with. But to the oblate who's singing loudly, out of tune, at Vigils. To the lawyer who's giving you hell because of the state of your only access road. To the heavens that regularly send down flames and, after the fire has loosened the topsoil, mudslides. One such catastrophe recently claimed twenty-three lives twenty minutes from my mother's house.

Now, as he veers at high speed down the twisty road in the storm, I look away from the edge, because it's so close. Used to navigating these uncertain paths in the dark, my friend is steering with one hand, as if he can drive it in his sleep (as, perhaps, he has done, often).

The rain pounds the windows and the wind rocks the old car back and forth. Most of the vehicles in the enclosure have long since been taken out of service; they can manage the short drive down to the mailbox at the foot of the hill, but not much more. Many lack even license plates.

"There's another slide that's going to take years to fix,"

he says as we speed along the empty road, debris scattered everywhere, rocks coming down to make us bounce. "It's just beneath our road. And there's the secondary road we have to build, in case of evacuations. We also need a new main road, the fire marshals are telling us." I can see nothing but his face, bright with hope and light.

"You don't seem very worried."

"God will take care of it."

We drive up to the restaurant, surrounded by yurts, set up—this is Big Sur—by a man who struck it rich by helping to make Teenage Mutant Ninja Turtle movies in the 1990s. A sushi chef serves up marvels some nights, but today there's only a huddle of souls, soggy and bedraggled, rubbing hands together to stay warm.

In the intimate quiet, I dare to ask, "What's the best thing about being in the cloister?"

He looks up to the ceiling, and says nothing for a long time. "Sometimes," he begins, "we can get really loud! The monks are coming from the north and from the south and we all get together in the refectory for lunch. It's deafening!"

"You miss your silence."

"No!" he says. "I love that sound! To have all your brothers there, laughing and talking. Getting another glass of wine or some more dessert." This is the great reward for all the trials of Job.

Opened up, he tells me of his time with his guitar every

day, the retreats he's scheduled to give, the books he's completing. He's on fire with the thought of kenosis, the practice of emptying oneself completely out. As we struggle back into the rain and get into the car to head home, he confides that by now his brothers need to raise five million dollars if they are going to have any chance for survival.

"But you never ask for money. You never seem desperate."

He smiles. The car lurches ever closer to the sheer drop on our left. Rocks keep tumbling down to make the road barely passable.

"It's almost as if, the more challenges you face, the more optimistic you become!"

"Everything will be all right in the end," says Cyprian, steering the car away from the precipice. "I fully believe that. If it's not all right, it's not the end."

He's following the narrow path through the dark as we turn off the empty highway and begin the slow, zigzagging trip up the hill.

"You can just see the lights through the mist," I say, looking up, to where people, robed and otherwise, are sitting in rich silence. Cyprian turns to me and, with a quiet smile, says, "Yes."

Acknowledgments

The soul evolves, Meister Eckhart tells us, not by addition but by subtraction. The same could be said of any book worth reading. In this case, my task was made more complicated by the fact that I'd assembled literally thousands of pages of notes over the first thirty-two years I spent in the New Camaldoli Hermitage, the most stimulating site I know; I began to feel most of my life was contained in them. And the challenge was deepened by my hope that I'd never come to an end of my relationship with that center of burning fragility, and that we'd continue spending time together as long as I was breathing.

My great companion in this fearsome task—or should I say, first victim?—was my faithful and unerring editor, Jynne Dilling Martin. She brought to this project not just her matchless diligence but her clear, keen sense that it

Acknowledgments

should be a book for every kind of reader, so long as it came from the depths. I was humbled yet again as she brought her liberating eye to every last adjective and semicolon, putting aside her own assumptions to help me clarify mine.

Everyone at Riverhead Books seems, in truth, a marvel of kindness, enthusiasm and fresh energy. With Geoff Kloske at the helm, I've received no end of help and support from tireless and always cheering Bianca Flores, Nora Alice Demick and Delia Taylor. I owe great thanks to Sheila Moody and Eric Wechter for taking exquisite care of the text. Lynn Nesbit, my old friend and agent, offered tremendous companionship and wisdom, and Miriam Feuerle, together with her colleague Abigail Parker, startled me daily by finding fresh ways for me to try to make a living. And in one of life's lovely surprises, my boyhood hero Jonathan Cott is now the friend who regularly sends me perfect books and poems, not least from Emily Dickinson.

It must be clear to anyone who's read this far how much I owe my "homies," as I think of both the monks and their many friends who've guided and inspired me for more than thirty years. As I write this, I see them proceeding into the chapel, one by one: Father Cyprian Consiglio, Father Raniero Hoffman, Father Isaiah Teichert, Father Zacchaeus Naegele, Father Bede Healey, Father Michael

Fish, Father Thomas Matus, Brother Michael Harrington, Father Daniel Manger, Father Arthur Poulin, Brother David Meyers, Father Ignatius Tully, Father Joseph Wong and many others who have passed through and lit up the space for weeks or years.

The fellow travelers I've met along the silent road above the sea are joined to me—and to one another—by what one can feel like the deepest and most durable of ties: I thank, for decades of friendship, Paula Huston, Paula Westphal, Deborah Smith Douglas, Lyn Farrugia, Chris and Debi Lorenc, John Marheineke, Mark and Diane Hansen, Vickie Conte and so many others, not least my longtime pals among the workers, Jack and Wade and Rick and John.

A monastery is in some ways a lab for coming to terms with loss, and many of those who've taught me so much are gone now: Father Robert Hale, who greeted me with such warmth soon after I arrived and was such a friendly companion over many lunches; Father Bruno Barnhardt, famous for his lyrical words and visionary insight; Brother Joshua Monson, who served us all lunch for twenty years or more with his soft *"Buon appetito"*; Brother Gabriel Kirby, who guided us in a shuttle van over the treacherous Road of Birth; Father Bernard Massicotte, who told me not to fear the mountain lion; Brother Emanuel Wasinger, who always said, whenever anyone saw him, "Still here."

Acknowledgments

Still here indeed, as are the late Ree Rickard, who brought the place to such vivid and embracing life for me, and the late Thérèse Gagnon, building her own sister church in the woods and illuminating the great chapel of the Outdoors. The late Brother Aelred-Seton Shanley, too, who sought me out because I'd written a book in youth about failing to be a monk.

It goes without saying how much I owe my life's partner in stillness, silence, our two-room flat and happy movement, Hiroko.

This book is about the beauty—you could say, the sanctity—of clarity and silence. It's also about how something of such treasure are available to us in many settings, not always monastic. What a joy, therefore, to be able to write so much of it in the transfiguring peace, amidst the constant stillness, of the Banff Centre for Arts and Creativity. Canada has long seen how much it can enrich its people by encouraging the arts, and among the snowcaps and sunlit lawns of the Banff Centre, in almost embarrassingly luxurious surroundings, I, like so many others, have been given the greatest of presents: the freedom to think, to wander and to lose myself in what's around me.

Thank heavens for such generosity, and such possibilities right at the heart of our confounding world.